Seasoned in Vermont

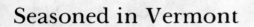

Seasoned in Vermont

Marguerite Hurrey Wolf

Illustrations by Sue Storey

The New England Press
Shelburne, Vermont

The New England Press
P.O. Box 525
Shelburne, Vermont 05482

Library of Congress Catalog Card Number: 82-80344
ISBN: 0-933050-11-9

*For Morgan Wolf Page, the only one of
us who was made in Vermont.*

PRINTED IN THE UNITED STATES OF AMERICA

Contents

Seasoned in Vermont

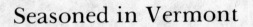

But What Do You Do in the Country?

Every time we go back to New York City we congratulate ourselves that we live in Vermont. We enjoyed Manhattan when
we lived there for fifteen years, but that was a long time ago.
In 1939 the subway cost five cents. The only graffiti was an
occasional moustache adorning a billboard picture. A soda at
Schraffts was twenty-five cents, and the movies at the local
movie houses cost fifty cents before six o'clock. George's tuition in medical school was eight hundred dollars a year, and
the rent for our apartment was fifty dollars a month. Of course,
my teaching salary peaked at two thousand per year after five
years of teaching, and we had no car, no life insurance, no tele-
vision, and no children for five years. But none of our friends
felt the need of those amenities either, so we didn't miss them.
We actually felt sorry for one intern who was independently
wealthy because he had a penthouse, two children, a maid, and
and a governess, and his life was regimented by all of them.

The city is still full of excitement—music and art and shiny
things—but it seems too dirty, too crowded, too expensive,
and too snarly, both in traffic and attitude. Most of all, life
in the city is too dependent, too far removed from the natural

sources of life. Having achieved a measure of self-sufficiency by raising our own vegetables, chickens, pigs, sheep, and geese, making our own maple syrup, and, to some extent, heating with our own firewood, we feel that the city offers more frustration than satisfaction.

It is true that in the country we need a car and a truck for transportation, but we can get to Burlington (eighteen miles) in twenty-five minutes. That would take three times as long, use twice the gas, and be an exhaust-filled trip in the city. When you can find a taxi with its flag up, it creeps along at the speed of a diesel in zero weather and takes three quarters of an hour to go the ten crosstown blocks.

In addition to semi-independence, we now are acutely aware of the environment and the infinite variety of Vermont's multiple seasons. Flower carts and the tunnel beds at Rockefeller Plaza do blossom in the spring, but you enjoy them as a spectator rather than as a participant. I plant every one of our bulbs with numb fingers on a cold November day, scolding myself for not having done it comfortably in October, but I feel a sense of personal achievement when the daffodil spears push up through the leaf mold in late March. I am in harness with nature, alternately shoving and pulling, but I am no idle bystander. The trees, even the maples in Central Park, do not put on the brilliant foliage display that excites us in Vermont. They just hang from the twigs in monochromatic apathy until they drift to the ground among the gum wrappers and beer cans. The sky in the city is something that releases unwelcome rain, snow, or soot, but it doesn't relay messages all day the way it does in the country.

I don't think man has progressed far enough from his primitive condition to be at peace with himself unless he is in actual touch with the land. Everything that feeds us, shelters us, and clothes us comes from the earth. If we don't protect it, nourish it, and help to make it productive, we will destroy not only the environment but ourselves. The decay of the cities is already apparent. It is, however, the erosion of the spirit, as well as the material deterioration, that is the contagion to be dreaded at the end of the twentieth century—much as yellow fever was dreaded at the end of the eighteenth.

When we get back in tune with the seasons, get our hands in the earth and smell the earliest scents of spring, we reverse the atrophy of our senses. This atrophy becomes necessary for survival in the city. You have to tune out the impact of all the different noises and faces, the poverty and distress, in order to maintain your emotional stability. You learn to ignore most of your environment. After we had lived in the city for a few years I was standing on the corner of Second Avenue one morning waiting to cross the street. After quite a few minutes I remember thinking, "I'll never get across there if those elephants keep coming." Elephants!! It had taken me that long to come alive to the fact that the circus was coming to town and the elephants were being marched down Second Avenue to Madison Square Garden. When I look out of our window here I notice that a red squirrel has different markings from the one swinging on the so-called squirrel-proof bird feeder.

In the country every day is filled with surprises. This morning I looked out of the living room window and saw that one of the geese was outside of the fence. By the time I got down there the gander had joined her on the greener side, and the next ten minutes was spent in a ridiculous tame-goose chase heading them off at assorted passes. When they were finally maneuvered back into their pasture, my self-esteem for having outwitted them (temporarily) lasted all morning. Then I found a pure white goose egg in a makeshift nest of dried grass and put it in my pocket—inasmuch as the goose didn't seem interested in brooding. George is addicted to deviled eggs, and one deviled goose egg serves two generously. Tiny amethyst and jade tips of asparagus were poking up through the moist earth in the vegetable garden, not of edible size but a promise. On a mossy bank at the edge of our road there is a tiny patch of trailing arbutus that I've been watching, and overnight the buds had opened. I knelt in the leafy mold to sniff the cool sweet fragrance of the furry pink blossoms. As I straightened up I heard the far-off baying chorus of Canada geese, the essence of wildness, and I could just pick out the wavering V formation of those "hounds of heaven" arrowing north over my head.

That's what you do in the country.

The Ambivalence of January

For some reason I always picture the calendar in the shape of a clock with January up at the top, moving much too slowly counterclockwise from 12 to 11. This clock is flat on top, and the plateau is January, named for that old, two-faced Roman god who kept the gates of heaven. He could look backward over the old year or forward to the new. The month of January is as two-faced as he was, full of contradictions. I've known it to be twenty below with the nails in the walls popping ominously at night and snow squeaking under your boots in the driveway. But you can also expect a January thaw, and one year, to the anguish of the skiers, it was mostly thaw and bare ground. Our confused daffodils on the south side of the house came up an inch. Fran Howe picked a snowdrop in her yard in Burlington, and the chipmunks came out from their snug bed-sitters on January 22 and poked around under our bird feeders to stuff a few sunflower seeds into their cheeks. The year before that the first chipmunk showed himself on April 22, three months later, for pity's sake! Of course, I know that chipmunks aren't true hibernators, but they usually do their winter stretching and snacking underground.

January is not one of my favorite months. You could stuff it down an empty woodchuck hole and leave it there until May, when I would welcome its thirty-one days as an extension of May. Wouldn't that be great, two months of dandelion-spangled meadows, lambs, lilacs, and apple blossoms? Our Vermont spring could become a season instead of an evanescence, and we'd never miss January at all.

January is one of the few months without a holiday to relieve the tedium of its thirty-one days. Well, there is New Year's Day, but doesn't that seem like the last of the Christmas holidays instead of a part of January? There is a movement afoot to make Martin Luther King's birthday a national holiday, and although it is not especially festive, it would be welcome and certainly deserved.

The ambivalent spirit of January infects us all. I start to clean out the closets, find a tarnished candlestick, and end up polishing the silver. One year we thought of going over to Lake Placid to watch the pre-Olympics and decided to go to Middlebury for lunch instead. We consider taking the Amtrak to Montreal for the day and then can't face the five hours on the train.

I am a sucker for the January sales, lured by the reduced prices more than I am restrained by the memory of that blouse I bought last January which languishes unworn in the closet.

We complain about the cold but boast that our thermometer read thirty below when the weatherman said it was only twenty in Burlington. If it is going to be cold, we want to claim the coldest. A neighbor's birch tree exploded, splitting right down the middle after a sudden drop in temperature, and he "stoppeth one of three" to tell about this phenomenon—just like the Ancient Mariner.

The Dutch used to call January *Lawumaand*, "frosty

month," and the Saxons, *Wulf-Monath* because wolves were more troublesome when food was scarce. Frosty is usually an understatement, and wolves no longer are troublesome in these parts. In the French calendar of the first French Republic it was called snow month, but in a typical Vermont winter we have five snow months if we are lucky and six if half of November is prematurely white and the first half of April can't kick the snowy habit.

If you live in California or Florida do you also come down with the January blahs out of tribal memory of the time when your ancestors lived in a four-season climate? I encounter so few native Floridians or Californians that they seem a maverick breed to me—like the native New Yorker who equates Vermont with Siberia. In New York when I gave my address to a salesgirl she asked how to spell Vermont and then said, "Is that a state?" I ought to have been sympathetic because we lived in Manhattan for fifteen years before we moved to Vermont, but during the last four of those years we had summered happily in Vermont and knew it was where we belonged.

I do know one true Floridian, Jane Rowley, but not only she lives in Florida—so did her mother, her grandmother, and her great-grandmother, all on the same lovely plantation on the St. Johns River.

I have learned that apple trees need the long cold rest period in order to produce good fruit. But woodchucks and jumping mice hibernate not because they need the deep sleep but because that is how they evolved to make it through the winter when their food supply has disappeared. I wish I could hibernate through January and lose a few pounds by living off my fat put on during the Christmas holidays because it would make January seem like one night instead of thirty-one long ones. One of the few good things about January is that the

9

days grow noticeably longer and seed catalogs brighten the mail box with their colorful, exaggerated promises of a bountiful and unblemished harvest.

And another bonus is the later afternoon light that suffuses the snow-covered mountains with a rosy glow. The pink snow only lasts a few minutes, but it seems a promise of returning light—which is what the regeneration of spring is all about. The evening grosbeaks add a touch of color, and the sight of one of our geese sitting on their waterer with curls of steam coming up around his ample body makes me laugh, but over all the kindest thing I can say for old Janus and his namesake month is good-bye till next year!

A Skunk by Any Other Name

I'll bet you have seen 100 dead skunks for every live one. Many people who are very familiar with what a skunk looks and smells like have never seen one in the wild. The nocturnal wanderings and appetite for carrion on the highways lure large numbers of *Mephitis mephitis* to death on the roads.

That name means bad smell times two, which I presume means that the smell is twice as bad as other odors. And if you are unfortunate enough to be in the line of fire the fumes can be nauseating as well as adhesive.

I can take skunks or leave them alone, but preferably the latter, and I hope the feeling is mutual. In fact, until recently our acquaintance with skunks had been sporadic and benign.

When Debbie, one of our daughters, was about six, we lived in South Burlington. We had a long driveway or lane leading down to our house from the highway. One afternoon she had been playing with her friend Muffy Brown and came home at dusk. I walked up the lane to meet Debbie and saw what I thought at first was one of our black and white cats walking in the center of the driveway. Debbie was skipping down the lane waving to me when I realized from the waddle and fluffy tail that the small beast between us was no kitty. Debbie was gaining on the skunk and in another minute might have scooped it up in her arms as was her wont with all our cats.

"Debbie," I yelped. "Stop!" She skipped merrily on.

"Go out in the field. That's a skunk."

At this strange request she paused with one foot in the air. So did the skunk. They regarded each other solemnly, and then Debbie made a wide circle out into the field. The skunk chose the opposite side of the lane and waddled off into the tall grass at top skunk speed, which isn't very fast.

Some years later Patty, our other daughter, had a close encounter with a skunk in Weston, Mass. One hot night she decided to sleep outdoors on the back terrace. Shortly before dawn she hurtled into the house reeking of skunk. He must have been startled by seeing her on the terrace and sprayed the area liberally, although none actually hit Patty.

My father had told me about an experience he had with a skunk when he was a boy. He grew up on a farm in Michigan that was similar to many Vermont farms. They raised cows, corn, and hay, tapped a sugar bush, and cut a woodlot. They burned wood in the parlor stoves and the big black range in the kitchen. It was my father's chore to fill the woodbox next to the range. One evening when he went out to get the kindling and split logs for the next morning, he heard something moving in the woodpile. He saw the rear end of a skunk protruding from between the logs. In the dim light from the kerosene lamp in the kitchen he could see that the skunk had his head stuck in a small cream can, which was jammed between two logs. He apparently had tried to get the last licks out of the cream can and then couldn't remove his head. With more brains than my father had hitherto attributed to a skunk, the small creature had wedged the can between the logs and was

now trying to extricate himself by wildly digging his heels into the earth and pulling. With a mighty heave and an audible grunt he pulled himself free, glared at my father as though it were all his fault, and scuttled off into the night. No hit, no miss, no error!

A few summers ago we set the Hav-a-hart trap next to the garden, hoping to deter our resident woodchuck from his nightly forays under the fence. The next morning I saw that there was something in the trap all right, but it didn't look like a woodchuck. It was smaller and very definitely black and white, peering out apprehensively at me as I peered in apprehensively at him. How do you remove a skunk from a trap without activating his defense mechanism? Not only was I not eager to touch him with a ten-foot pole, an eleven-foot pole lacked appeal. So I did what I often do when confronted with unforseen country crises—waited for George to come home. He tried to lift the end of the trap with the long handle of our outside window-washing squeegee, but the trap tipped over on its side. He flipped it over again and lifted the bar so that the catch came loose. We beat a hasty retreat, and when we returned the skunk had left without a trace of scent.

Last summer when Patty and I sat on our deck in the sun, we both noticed a faint odor of skunk. We peered through the spaces between the boards of the deck but didn't see anything in the gloomy recesses beneath it. We decided a skunk must be or have been under there, but discretion seemed the better part of valor and we didn't hunt further. In December we smelled skunk one evening, opened the door, and then shut it very quickly. The odor was overpowering, and it was definitely coming from under our porch. We decided our cat must have invaded the privacy of the skunk's winter quarters, but the cat didn't smell skunky at all. The pervasive scent lasted not just for days but for weeks, waxing and waning in strength. When our cat subsequently went to the great catnip field in the sky we expected the skunk spraying program to end. Not at all. In the utility room off the porch it was eye-watering in intensity.

I consulted assorted naturalists who said the skunks would move out in the spring. But what will keep them from moving back next winter and the next and the next? Moth balls were suggested. I bought a box, crushed them and stuffed them through the cracks in the porch floor. I'm not crazy about the smell of moth balls, but given the choice I suppose I prefer it to skunk scent. If anything, the moth balls acted as a stimulant. Perhaps they roused the skunk from his shallow winter sleep. I can only attest to the fact that one strong pungent odor does not cancel out one that is equally aggressive. We now reek of both skunk and moth balls.

I know what you are going to suggest because you are not the first. Swabbing down decks with water is one thing, but tomato juice aging in the wood would only add a third dubious fragrance and compound the felony. I'll wait for spring, which is a panacea for most winter ailments.

What's a Vermonter?

In the June 28, 1981, Sunday *Burlington Free Press,* Brian Vachon, editor of *Vermont Life,* wrote a perceptive article on the non-Vermonter, that species "from away" who has been infiltrating Vermont in increasing numbers in the last few decades. Of course, that shows that the non-Vermonter has good taste, but some of his other tastes in food, dress, and metropolitan habits are definitely not indigenous to the Green Mountain State.

I agree with Brian's description of the non-Vermonter. He sadly admits that he is not a born Vermonter. Neither am I, but I do have one foot firmly in the door by virtue of the fact that I had two great-grandfathers who were native Vermonters and who lived in West Brattleboro when the state was just establishing its identity. Unfortunately, they were on the wrong side politically, being Tories as were many southeastern Vermont families at that time. Walter Hard, Sr. admitted to me that his ancestors were also Tories, but you'd never hesitate to call him a Vermonter. My other credential for picking up the gauntlet and presuming to describe the Vermonter is that we've paid taxes here since 1948 and raised animals, vegetables, and children in Chittenden County—so I'm not a Jane-come-very-lately.

16

First of all, a Vermonter doesn't give a darn about where or if you went to prep school or college, or if you are listed in the *Social Register*. Your worth is measured by your performance, by your ability to keep your mouth shut more often than it is open, and by your affinity for hard work and mending your own fences. The Vermonter will never give you advice. In fact, if you ask him for advice you will rarely get a definitive answer because he assumes that what you do is your business whether you stoke your stove with white pine or pick blackberries in short sleeves.

He eyes with a certain amount of suspicion the person "from away" who leaps into Vermont politics and wants to pave the state in the form of shopping centers or put up a condominium on the family farm. He has no intention of pointing out the pitfalls because it is more fun to watch the non-Vermonter fall into them.

The Vermonter speaks an idiom not heard on the corner of 42 Street and Fifth Avenue. He does not work for you, he "helps out," and at his convenience, not yours. He eats creamed dried beef but calls it dried beef gravy. The thought of carrots, onions, or potatoes nestling under the crust of his chicken pie is as shocking as putting tomatoes in clam chowder. The famous Parker House product is not rolls—they are biscuits. Pies are made at home, not purchased frozen at the supermarket. So is ketchup, and it is darker and sweeter than Mr. Heinz's condiment. Syrup, of course, means maple and not cane or any variation thereof.

If he is not "out straight" with his own chores and "hays it" for you or plows your garden, the Vermonter may very likely not send a bill. When your conscience nudges you into pressing for a settlement, he goes into a trance, looks uncomfortable, and murmurs, "Will $20 be all right?" If he is more

17

than forty, he wears a long-sleeved shirt and pants when haying. If he is more than sixty, he may wear a "frock" over his overalls. No, that's not a woman's dress. Remember the picture of Calvin Coolidge haying on his father's farm? That's a frock.

He doesn't go downtown, he goes "down street." He "does his trading" one day a week, usually on Friday. He does not buy wheat germ, sesame oil, yogurt, or ginger root unless his children have converted him. He wouldn't think of buying maple syrup or ham at Harrington's even though he may have known Luke and Mary Harrington as neighbors. If he doesn't boil his own syrup and raise his own pig, he gets both on shares from a neighbor or buys them at the supermarket. He plants his garden on Memorial Day. Even a "couple, three" days later or "such a matter" he "mistrusts" could do any harm.

He observes five sacred holidays: Christmas, Easter, the first day of trout fishing, Bennington Battle Day, and the first day of deer hunting. If he's lucky he doesn't get "a deer," he gets "his deer."

That he is taciturn is a myth. He lets you do most of the talking until he sizes you up, but once he starts telling you about "the time when," his terminal facilities are very poor. He knows more about you in a week than you will ever know about him, but he will never tell you what to do. If you paint your house in the middle of winter or when the siding is wet, he figures it is your house. If you are laid up the Vermonter will do your chores, bring in a covered dish, and plow your driveway because that's the way it is always done. He takes it for granted that you would do the same for him. You'd better if you hope to lose the stigma of the non-Vermonter in a generation or so.

He can't imagine wanting to live anywhere else in the world, and neither can I.

18

February

There is an old proverb that says,

"February fill dyke, be it black or be it white
But if it be white, it's the better to like."

I agree. The ground as well as the dyke in February looks better snow-covered than bare and bleak as it was in the winter of 1980. Somehow all the debris of winter that surfaces in March when the snow recedes to granular fringes is tolerable then only because you know that spring is imminent and thrusts of green will soon camouflage the winter-weary landscape. But in February you know those sodden leaves, the odd mitten, beer cans, and candy wrappers will be mercifully covered with snow again only to make a second appearance before spring cleaning fever is upon us.

The ancient Romans called it the month of purification, and the name comes from *februo,* "I purify by sacrifice." Our February rituals, Valentine's day and Washington and Lincoln's birthdays are hardly sacrificial or purifying, but in the wild this is the hunger month and a good many animals are sacrificed to starvation in a normal February. The winter of 1980 was so bare and snowless that the deer herds flourished. The ones who were making the unwilling sacrifice were the owners

19

of ski resorts and all their ancillary services, such as motels and restaurants. But purification was not noticeable in their colorful laments that February.

The Anglo-Saxons called February *sprout-kale* for the early appearance of cabbage and kale, but the English climate is considerably warmer in February than that in Vermont. The only thing sprouting in Vermont in February is an occasional pussywillow or a misguided snowdrop on the south side of the house, next to the chimney. On the bays of Lake Champlain ice-fishing shanties sprout, and in the days before electrical refrigeration, that was the time to cut the ice for storage. When the ice was 12 inches thick it was cut in blocks of 12 by 12 by 24. The first cut was plowed by horse power and then sawed in blocks by hand. When I was a child we summered in Maine, and one of our favorite occupations on a hot day was to go to the ice house and dig down through the damp redolent sawdust until we unearthed a cake of ice. As I recall we sat on it or chipped off bits to suck. We had to be careful, however, to cover the exposed cakes with sawdust before we sneaked out because excavating in the ice house was frowned upon by our parents.

Drawing wood was a February chore because the logs could be snaked out over the snow by the horses. Now that almost every Vermont home has sprouted a woodpile, the hills are alive with the sounds of chainsaws. Their racket would be more tolerable if it didn't sound so much like the snowmobiles that pollute our silent woods with their noise and fumes.

Our bird population increases in February. This year the purple finches arrived February 20 to join the chickadees, nuthatches, woodpeckers, and evening grosbeaks. A treeful of bluejays, lemon-colored evening grosbeaks, and raspberry-tinted purple finches does a lot to lift the spirit on a gray February morning. The chickadees are now repeating "spring soon," and one or two optimistic neighbors have hung their sap buckets by the last week in February. But the most noticeable is the increasing light. The quality of the afternoon light is altogether different from January: night no longer falls like a cold ax. The golden glow washes over the west side of every white farmhouse and church steeple, tinting them pale yellow in sharp contrast to the thundercloud blue of the lengthening shadows. The snow-covered mountains are ignited briefly with rose fading softly to shell pink, pearl gray, and then blue, as night settles gently, wrapping the land in a blanket that may be the coldest of the year. It is in February that Lake Champlain freezes over if it is going to, and the thermometer may slink down to 20 below before dawn. But, as Gladys Taber says, "The yeast of spring is in the air." The birds know it. The buds on the trees respond to the increasing light and swell perceptibly on the lilac twigs. Red osier stems glow crimson along the roadsides.

The stirring has begun. Far down in the woodchuck holes there is movement, and although the winter sleep may not be over, it is now restless and intermittent. The raccoon prowls at night hunting for a mate. An occasional chipmunk pokes his head out of a hole to test the air and stuff his cheeks with sunflower seeds, and the winter-lean raccoon climbs up a tree and out on a limb to steal the suet from our bird feeder.

As the woodpiles and the snowdrifts shrink, down underneath more than a foot of snow the snowdrops respond to the filtered warmth and begin reaching toward the light, undaunted by the weight of the snow; they thrust up pale green blades that may not surface until March. It is a beginning, a promise—perhaps not to be fulfilled for almost a month—that after the purification and the sacrifice of winter, spring will surely come.

21

Spare Ribs, Country Style

This has nothing to do with pork. I'm talking about Adam's spare rib, the one that turned into Eve, the original country wife. Eve had no choice between urban and country living. No one had nightmared up cities at that time, so she was a country wife willy-nilly.

When I became a country wife it was willy even though my skills in coping with rural life were definitely nilly. When we moved to Vermont to become "year-round summer folk" nearly thirty years ago, my skills were in dealing with metropolitan life. I know which cross streets went east and west, how to change from the BMT to the IRT, and which days the museums were closed. In my experience it had always been summer in the country. I had a Red Cross life-saving badge and knew how to paddle a canoe and dig clams at low tide. What I did not know was how to load a pig, wallpaper a room that was plastered circa 1820, cull a laying hen, shoot a gun, and other skills too numerous to mention. I still don't know how to shoot because the gun slips out of my hands when I put my fingers in my ears. The wallpapering I have long since put behind me to the improvement of our interior decoration because I never mastered the art of pasting, folding, and flipping a strip onto the wall without having it come alive and wrap around my head and shoulders sticky side down. My first attempt was the dining room of our old house in Jericho. Lacking a wallpapering board, I laid the strips, smeared with paste, out on the floor. I thought the children were busy playing outdoors, but with that unerring knack for surfacing where you'd rather they didn't, three-year-old Debbie ran into the room. Her small sneakered feet briefly touched the slick end of a long strip of pasted wallpaper and she skidded on the seat of her overalls the length of the room and bounced off the far wall. After that my wallpapering became an evening occupation—after the children were asleep. But nobody told me that in a very old house the distance between the ceiling and floor may be different at different spots around the room. A country wife learns to measure each strip, one at a time. This dining room had four windows and four doors of all varying sizes and inclinations. That had not been true in our city apartments. The management painted it every other year in those days.

The care and feeding of automobiles is another cause that a country wife does well to espouse. Like worrying about something that then seems to prevent it from happening, ever since I learned how to change a tire and rock a car out of a snowbank, I've never had to do either one. When we first came to Vermont in the summer and my husband was working in New York during the week, he thought I should learn how to change a tire. So one warm July Sunday, after showing me the necessary parts, he sprawled out on the lawn, chewing on a timothy stem, while I struggled with a temperamental jack, recalcitrant lugs, and a dirt-encrusted tire. One or two cars went past, but we were still too urban to realize that in the country everyone is interested (no, not nosey, interested) in what their neighbors are doing. Several weeks later George was in the village garage and heard one local man say to the garage owner, "That's him, the fellow who just lay on the grass doing nothing while he made his wife change the tire!"

For at least six months of the year I do use my acquired gardening skills. It is a recurrent miracle to me that those seed packets contain the potential for a lush, productive garden. Six flat pumpkin seeds burgeon into a tentacled jungle with enormous orange blossoms and leaves the size of elephant ears. Three plants of zucchini produce more than a hundred squash. Seed potatoes multiply by five, and I'm still child enough to feel like it is Easter morning when we pull up the potato plants and see whole clusters of tubers hanging by their roots.

But I began gardening simply as an unskilled laborer. I had a Jack-O-Lantern in mind when I planted a whole packet of Connecticut field pumpkins the first year and felt like Atlas when I tried to stagger up from the garden with one monster on my shoulder. I planted the whole envelope of parsley seed and was hard pressed to find uses for the resulting green hedge. I tried to beat the system by transplanting tomato and pepper plants at the same time that I was told all Vermont gardens were planted, Memorial Day, and I had to replant when we had a killing frost on June 10. Now I plant succession plantings of lettuce, beans, carrots, and beets, and we enjoy early and late crops.

But country living isn't all smelling the roses and that strange pungent scent of tomato leaves. Along with the flora you face the pleasures and perils of fauna too, both wild and domestic. The wild we try to discourage, and the domestic we nurture to the best of our limited ability and energy. Many people in Vermont raise sheep for fun and profit. We tried it, and we didn't like it. A lamb is a creature of beauty and charm but it rapidly turns into a dirty, stupid sheep. Sheep require a lot of tender loving care. The shepherdess has to be willing to ram worm pills down their throats routinely, reach into the other end on occasion at lambing time, transport them to be shorn and bred every time unless you keep a ram. And if you do keep a ram he is no one to trifle with unless you wear padded clothing. At butchering time, even if you send off the hides to be cleaned and tanned, you still have to rub salt into the wet skins for three or four days, curing and drying your skin as well as that of the sheep.

Pigs, on the other hand, are wonderful, and the country wife would do well to put aside any preconceived notions she has about them. They are funny when they are little, relatively immune to diseases (in twenty years of pig raising we've had one sick pig), totally dedicated to the pursuit of happiness through oral gratification, clean if given the opportunity, and the best money savers on a small farm. Our completely grain-fed pork in the fall of 1980 came to less than one dollar a pound. And that includes the cost of the piglets, all the grain, the shavings for their bedding, and the fees for butchering and curing and smoking the meat. I suppose if you aspired to being a complete country wife you would help with the butchering, curing, and smoking and would render all the fat and make head cheese and blood sausage. Those are the parts I can do without. I love raising pigs and I've even acquired a reputation for pig loading (more from writing about it than from skill), but we are quite happy to have Andy Abair come and do in our pigs each fall. In one hour he shoots, bleeds, debristles, hangs and eviscerates the carcasses and even takes away "the inwards."

This year, while the water was heating (in the heater he

25

brings) to fill the tub (which he also brings) in which to immerse the pigs, he paused to eat lunch in the cab of his truck. I went down to ask him something and couldn't believe the scene in the cab. Andy is probably about 6' 3" and must weigh 250 pounds. In his winter clothing and rubber overalls he looks like a Sumo wrestler dressed for the slopes. It hardly seems possible that he can squeeze behind the wheel of his pick up. But that front seat contained Andy, his wife, a picnic lunch, and something else that was alive. Perched on Andy's large knee was a miniature feather duster of a dog, a Chi-Poo, half-Chihuahua and half-poodle, prancing on its tiny hind legs, begging for scraps of meat from Andy's sandwich.

Chickens and geese are fun and functional. When we first came to Vermont I took Donald Henderson's course in poultry raising at the University of Vermont. I studied conscientiously (I find you do when you pay your own tuition). You would think I would have developed some expertise in running a model chicken house. Well, think again. Our chicken "house" is improvised from part of the cow barn. George invented a feeder and built the nests and roost onto the side walls. After he had finished building the nesting suite, he called me down to admire his work. With a sheepish grin he pointed out that although the hinged lid lifted beautifully to allow the humans to extract the eggs from the nests, he had forgotten to cut an entrance for the hens to get into the nests! He cut them a door and a nice little entrance ramp and it all works perfectly. Well, not perfectly—there is no such adverb in the country. We still have to wage war against rats even though the stored feed is in covered containers: there is always some left in the feeders overnight.

If your venture into the Garden of Eden includes keeping laying hens you'd better learn how to cull the poor layers.

26

Even under the tutelage of Mr. Henderson the curve of my success is wavy. It's a blow to the poultrywoman's ego to dress off a hen and find her full of eggs of all sizes, from tiny little golden globules to big jumbo-size ones with the skin on, ready to go. You feel like you've killed the goose that laid the golden egg and you probably have. But you do feel superior to your city sisters when you can upend a biddy, measure the distance between her pelvic bones, look at the color of her legs and size of her comb. and pronounce judgment on her future. Hens are comforting. There is something soothing about their murmuring and clucking. I find myself talking back to them companionably, in girl talk.

If you aspire to be a ten in country-wifery, you really should learn to split wood. At the time when we first moved to Vermont, fossil fuels weren't threatened with extinction. Can you believe we sold the woodburning parlor stove that we found in our old house for five dollars because we didn't think we'd have any use for it? If you have a resident woodsman you may not need a woodswoman. My doubtful help on the other end of a two man saw convinced George that a chain saw was cheaper than a divorce. Just as well to be inept in a few areas. Your help will still be enlisted in stacking, lugging, and disposing of the fine film of motes and beams that float around and finally come to rest on the furniture.

The long-time country wives of Vermont in my age bracket whom I admire more frequently that I emulate know how to milk cows, drive tractors, load a hay wagon, and can several hundred jars of home-grown fruits and vegetables. The new breed of young ex-urbanite is more likely to milk a goat if she fancies the role of milkmaid. She has a large garden and freezes most fruits and some vegetables. She makes pickles and jellies and gloats over their abundance in her kitchen. She

27

may even spin and weave the wool from her own sheep. The choices are multiple, and so are the rewards. Who says the spirit of the pioneer woman is obsolete? It is alive and well in Vermont. She may once have been called Adam's rib, but she has learned from Eve's mistake. She has sent the snake packing, made the untouched apple into applesauce, and plans to settle down right where she is, in the Garden of Eden.

March

In New Jersey, where I grew up, or in western Massachusetts, where I went to college, March meant early spring, fat daffodil buds pushing out of their overlapping green sheaths, robins all over lawns that were studded with crocuses in the traditional Easter colors, purple and yellow. And later on when we lived in Kansas City, March was full-blown spring with magnolias, cottage tulips, fountains of forsythia, and redbud trees turning the handsome suburbs into a series of Easter-card scenes, which also came from the Hallmark headquarters in Kansas City.

But here in Vermont we have to scratch around in the sodden leaves to find spring in March. It is true that the maple trees sprout sap buckets and the juncos arrive at our bird feeders on their way north. Pussy willows fuzz out tenderly, but for the most part March is a boisterous, noisy, muddy month, a contrast of snowstorms (our biggest blizzards are usually in March), winds that send the bird feeders leaping and dancing around, pelting rain, and the occasional lovely, warm, clear day that feels like May as long as you stay in the sun. The minute you step into the shade you know that winter hasn't let go quite yet.

And the wind! Some people like the wind. My mother used to feel exhilarated by it and enjoyed seeing the flags trying to tear loose from the flagpoles and the sheets flapping and slapping wildly on the clothesline. I don't. It make me uneasy and apprehensive that something is going to blow down or away. And it often does. Our satellite bird feeder just sailed out into the pine trees and the front door blew open and slammed so hard against the house wall that some canned goods fell off the shelf in the utility room. Dead branches hurtle through the air, and birds' feathers are ruffled backward.

March just comes on too strong to be endearing. But when March stops roaring for a moment to catch its breath for another tantrum, the promises of spring can be found emerging timidly from the thawing ground. If you get down on your knees to poke among the wet leaves and release a daffodil spear that has impaled two or three dead leaves on its way up, you can smell spring—wet earth, rotting leaves, new growth. The snowdrop is my favorite because it is undaunted by March's vagaries. Near our front door the snow accumulates in a high drift, and because it is on the north side of the house it doesn't shrink totally away until late March. But the minute the miniglacier of blackened ice recedes, there are four or five snowdrops, perfectly erect and bright green with the tiny white bell ready to pop open.

About this time, if we flick on the outside light around nine o'clock at night, we may catch a raccoon standing on his hind legs and reaching up to scoop out the bacon fat from a log bird feeder. He licks his little handlike paw and digs in again with his probing black fingers. It always surprises me that instead of fleeing, he looks at us calmly and only humps off into the woods if we go outside. We have one bird feeder that is right on the windowsill, and chickadees and red squirrels will get in it and calmly go on eating even if I have my face two inches away on the inside of the glass. But if I just open the door, Whisk! they are off. How do they know that the pane of glass protects them?

We are ambivalent in our feelings about the raccoons. Not true hibernators, they occasionally will come out of their dens during a warm spell in the winter but by March are fully awake, at least at night; hungry from the long sleep of winter and finding slim pickings in the still half-frozen mud banks, they visit our bird feeders, making off with the suet if they can get it down and digging around under the feeders for spilled sunflower seeds. They are fun to watch. I love their masked faces, shoe-button eyes, and black rubber noses. They look more like toys than wild animals, but when our corn is just about ripe, they are a real nuisance. There have been summers when we got no corn and they had it all. We now have pretty well kept them out of the garden with fencing and an electric wire a few inches above the fence.

So it's a love-hate, or rather a charmed-annoyed, relationship, and we feel that it wouldn't be fair to feed them in the spring only to inhibit, trap, or shoot them in August.

Last week we saw our first raccoon of the season tasting the bacon fat at the log. I had forgotten that our other log was sitting on the table on the screened porch waiting for me to fill it. During the evening I heard some sounds outside, but when I looked out the window there was no raccoon in sight. Later I heard thumping again and opened the door to the porch. On the rock that juts into the porch sat the biggest raccoon I've seen, who immediately galumphed around the walls hunting for an exit. I wanted to open the screen door to let him out but he couldn't wait. There was a small mouse-size hole in the screen, and he plunged through that, ripping it

31

open to raccoon size and also to a size that will require a whole new panel. This didn't do much to endear him to George, so the Hav-A-Hart trap was set up near the bird feeders and baited with cracked corn.

Sure enough, the next morning the trap was totally filled with a live coonskin coat. He had reached between the bars and scratched a moat all the way around the trap and his mate or brother had valiantly dug several big holes under the trap to try to rescue him. I wish I'd seen that going on and heard their trilling and chirping, but we sleep through most of the drama that is enacted around our house every night. Shooting a trapped animal doesn't appeal much to George's sense of sportsmanship, though he has been known to do it during the corn season. None of our neighbors would welcome an addition to their already burgeoning raccoon population, so George put the trap in the back of the truck and we drove way up the mountain well beyond the last house before we opened the trap.

The raccoon wouldn't budge. Everytime we propped open the ends of the trap they would fall shut, so we tipped the trap on its side with one end open and out scrabbled that ball of coonskin at top speed. Up he scuttled over a snowbank, waddled across a partly wooded field, and headed straight up the sheer granite cliffs of Bolton Notch. He never looked back as a startled raccoon often does. He never slowed his pace and he climbed up and up, zigzagging where he could find crevices and footholds but always higher until we could no longer see him behind some bushes 300 feet above us. It was almost bittersweet watching him go, so handsome, so wild, so perfectly adapted to that rugged terrain.

And the next night, I flicked on the outside light and there was another raccoon poking his fingers into the refilled holes of the log. No it wasn't the same one. Their home territory is usually no more than two square miles, and we had relocated the first one at least five miles up the road. But was it his mate or the friend who had tried to help him escape? We reset the trap, which was sprung but empty the next morning. Perhaps this one was more suspicious. Raccoons are very clever, and we've often know them to reach in and extricate the bait while propping up the end of the trap with their high furry rumps, whether purposely or not, to prevent the trap from closing.

Raccoons are part of March when the awakening and the hunger and quest for a mate brings them out of their snug winter quarters to start the whole new cycle of life and growth that is spring.

Tossing Down
the Verbal Gauntlet

March is a warmonger. In the north country it is an alternation of snow, wind, rain, and a promise of spring that doesn't come true. Winter weary dispositions grow brittle, and words fly through the air that are never heard in June. There are several conversational openers that should be outlawed in the interest of détente if not lasting peace.

"Why must you always . . ." is equivalent to waving a red flag in front of an irritable bull. Another starter guaranteed to lose friends and alienate relatives is, "The trouble with you is . . . ." Most of us are quite aware of our shortcomings and our performance would be more likely to improve if we were met with, "One of the nice things about you is . . . ." Ask any woman and you'll find that the ultimate call to battle coming from her husband is "You are just like your mother." Now her mother may wear a halo six days out of seven, but those words don't refer to her saintly qualities. They do not mean, "You are just as kind as your mother." The imply that you are just as stuck in your ways or garrulous or nasty neat.

Unfortunately, the husband and wife exchanges are not the only ones. As soon as a child's vocabulary gets beyond "Da da" and "Bye, bye," the next pearls to drop from his little lips will likely be "Me first," "He started it," or "I'm going to tell Mommy."

When he gets a little older he automatically starts any promotional campaign with "Everybody else has," followed chronologically by "a two wheeler," "designer jeans," and "Head skis."

It's not necessarily true, of course, because a little parental research will prove that "everybody" is simultaneously voicing the same lament to his parents, relying heavily on the power of plural pressure.

I'll admit that some of these openers do at least show a breadth of vocabulary that previously seemed limited to "y'know," "Oh Wow!" and "Gross," but they are still incendiary and almost never have the desired effect. How often are the words, "Mom, absolutely everybody in my class is living in a separate pad instead of at home," followed by, "What a great idea. Find an apartment and we'll gladly pay the rent?" Unfortunately, there are a few parents who *would* gladly pay the rent to escape the litany of deprivation and the hassle of living in conflict with teenagers.

The situation isn't new. The cave kids wanted a heavier cudgel and a saber-toothed-tiger skin. But some of the desired objects change. Sneakers have been replaced by Adidas, Levis by Calvin Klein jeans, and the second-hand jalopy by wheels that have power everything.

I'm glad that I'm not young anymore. Now our children can worry about what our grandchildren are going to consider essential to life, liberty, and the pursuit of happiness. When our grandson Morgan, who is just about getting up on his hind legs at present, comes home sometime in the future saying, "Hey Dad, everybody is going to the moon over Christmas vacation," I hope Steve checks out "everybody" before he gives him money for green cheese. If not, his instinctive reaction could be, "The trouble with you is . . . ," or "You're just like your mother . . . ," or more appropriately, "You always want the moon!"

The Road Less Traveled By

"Four seasons fill the measure of the year," Keats wrote in his poem "Human Seasons." That may be true in England, but in Vermont we have a fifth season whose name is mud. Neither winter nor spring, it combines the least desirable elements of both. It can start in March, as it did this year, when we had such an untimely thaw that the daffodils started up only to be buried again under eight inches of snow. But daffodils are not all that comes up—so does the frost.

Although I have gone on record as preferring the back roads, this is the time of year when I'd rather leave them alone than take them. The roads heave and sink in patterns so bizarre that driving on them is like maneuvering an obstacle course guaranteed to instigate or reactivate lower back pain and test your car's shocks and springs beyond the call of duty.

You expect ruts when the frost comes out of the ground and tires gouge tracks in the soft earth. But the unexpected potholes, even on the paved highways, that may be as big as manhole covers and a foot deep catch you off guard and rearrange your vertebrae.

The road crews plow and scrape when they can and dump

endless loads of sand and gravel on the most offensive spots, which the receptive earth swallows and then waits for more. Sometimes the thermometer takes a plunge, and all the ruts and potholes freeze in their distorted shapes, to stay that way until the next thaw relaxes them.

It is no wonder that most Vermont houses have a mud room. When our children were little I was thankful that we had an extra room between the house and the garage where even if boots were not sloughed off as they were supposed to be, a good part of the mud was. No child can stay upright for long in the mud season, and their snowsuits used to be so plastered with mud that the only remedy was to let their outer clothing dry and then brush it off.

Puddles are magnetic to the young not just for walking through, but stamping in. The greater the splash, the greater the satisfaction. Debbie used to come in after playing, soaking wet, shivering, and smiling broadly.

In the 1920s and '30s our neighbor Rollin Tilley used to pull three or four cars out of the mud in front of his house every day in mud season. A team of horses or a tractor could get some traction, but those newfangled contraptions that were coming out of Detroit were bogged down up to their hubcaps.

If you live in a house by the side of the road in Vermont you have no choice but to be a friend to man, woman, and teenagers of indiscriminate sex. You really can't tell when they are dressed in heavy parkas and boots unless they are bearded. We hear the tires spinning and the engines laboring and know that in a few minutes someone will knock on the door and ask to use the phone. In the winter when the roads are icy they have usually gone off the road. In the mud season they have sunk into it.

38

When John Masefield wrote "It is good to be out on the road," he wasn't talking about Vermont in the fifth season. Mercifully it doesn't last, however; the road men stuff the potholes and dig culverts, and when the crows come out of the woods and the frost heaves sink back into their normal, relatively smooth surface, you know that spring is more than an empty promise.

April

Living through April is like swinging on a pendulum between the last chill clutch of winter and the warm promise of summer. It is the unfolding of spring, shy and tentative. There is a mist of green caught in the bare gray poplar branches. The maple sap stops running when the small, red flower buds appear. Vermont has so many maples that the hills from a distance seem to be suffused in soft rosy red, a pastel remembrance of the flaming October color. Today I picked a maple blossom and really looked at it for the first time in my life. It is a lovely little sunburst, made up of four flowerets, each of which has five petals and five long stamens. The color of the petals is claret red. It is the color that in my childhood paintbox was called madder lake. I remember because it seemed such a funny name for a color. Madder lake evoked no colors in my mind the way the words crimson or scarlet did. Sometimes it was called rose madder, and that was better but still not as evocative as American Beauty red, for instance.

There are many reds in April. The new twigs on old apple trees, the deep crimson shine of the osiers, the first tendrils of the sensitive ferns, and the rose to amethyst tips of asparagus that really shouldn't be poking up out of the ground inviting frostbite. Tight curled rhubarb leaves are green fists on fat red stalks, and slender wine-red spears of peonies repeat the same color in the flower garden.

April is full of beginnings. Our ewe is about to lamb. Our African geese began to lay on April 4 in the old tire filled with straw that George had provided. It you are conditioned to hen's eggs, as most of us are, a goose egg doesn't look like a zero. It looks like it is the product of an itinerant ostrich.

Now and then in April when the sun has some warmth at midday, it begins to smell like spring. The moist earth exudes a thin fragrance of growing things. The earliest flowers, snowdrops, crocuses, and tiny wild pansies, have such a faint fragrance that you have to get your nose covered with pollen to smell it. Crocus pollen, from a different variety, is the source of saffron, but there is no hint of the bitterness of saffron in this scent. It is thin, pure, and partly in the nose of the eager sniffer.

About the middle of April we drove down to the Morgan Horse Farm in Weybridge to see the mares and foals. There were three very young foals with their mothers, prancing, frisking, and galloping the length of their paddock at top speed. Nothing is more symbolic of youth, exuberance, and joie de vivre than a week-old foal. Lambs, foals, daffodils, forsythia, rhubarb, and asparagus, all fresh and bursting with life. Dandelions are just at the right stage of immaturity for salad, when the flower bud is just a nubbin. Mixed with store lettuce it tastes exactly like endive with just a slight bitter edge and has the distinct advantage of being free rather than three dollars a pound.

In mid-April we plant a few things in our small salad garden—onion sets, lettuce, radishes, and spinach—with the super-

41

vision of the ewe, two geese, and a white-throated sparrow, all in full voice. Our main garden is still much too wet and has to wait until at least mid-May.

By the end of the month the shadbush will be in bloom and there will appear a few patches of bluets on south sloping pastures. The shadbush blooms at the same time that the shad move up the rivers in some parts of the country, and if I were there and if a pair of shad roe did not cost three times the price of porterhouse steak, I would celebrate April with a gourmet meal of shad roe and bacon, fresh buttered asparagus, and rhubarb pie!

Oh Rats!

It was almost 700 years ago that the Pied Piper exterminated the rats of Hamelin. And in all that time no one has ever matched the efficiency of his method. Of course it was expensive for Hamelin in the long run because the mysterious piper in a parti-colored suit ultimately lured away all the children as well after the village fathers refused to pay him the contracted sum for his services. This may also have been related to the story of the children's crusade, which took place in 1212. That, too, was a fiasco. The 40,000 German children led over the Alps by Nicholas didn't get any nearer to the Holy Grail than Italy.

I wish the Pied Piper would turn up again, this time in Jericho. We do see occasional mysterious young men in bizarre clothing, but they don't show any noticeable enthusiasm for rats. Hardly anyone does. Rats are not lovable, except to other rats, but they are far from being an endangered species. Like those birthday candles which relight themselves when you blow them out, they are almost unextinguishable. We know because we've been trying to rat-proof our barn for a year and a half. We get results all right: we have trapped or killed

218. How many more, done in by D-Con, have breathed their last somewhere where we haven't found them, I don't know. If we could lift our barn off its reclining foundation, I'm sure we'd see evidence of a rat colony of heroic proportions.

Why is our barn so attractive to rats? Because it is also home to twenty-five hens and two pigs. The pigs clean up their food within minutes, so they don't leave any bits for the rats. The feed is stored in covered galvanized metal trash cans. But the chickens have a long narrow feeder that always has some residual mash in it. You're supposed to keep the feed in front of them all the time, aren't you? It would be above and beyond the call of duty to go down every evening and scoop out the last bit of feed and then return before daylight to refill it. The hens get up on their roosts as soon as it is dark. You've heard of going to bed with the chickens. But they start eating again at the crack of dawn, and I'm not eager to rush down there at 4:30 in the morning in the summer or mush through the snow at 7:00 in the winter.

We keep the hens more for fun than for profit. The cost of feed has eliminated the profit, and it is more fun to feed the animals after we've had our own breakfast. So the rats of lower Nashville Road enjoy an all-night cafeteria and grow fat and fertile at our expense. Norway rats have a gestation period of 21 days and produce 8 to 10 rats per litter. They may have as many as 10 litters a year, so even without a calculator you can see that we are not even keeping up with their fecundity. Lord knows how many breeding females we are harboring. If we have only 10 mamas under the barn and each one produces 80 to 120 ratlets a year, their increase is way ahead of our current ability to trap or poison them.

Hammacher Schlemmer advertizes an ultra-sonic rat elimi-nator for $159.95. "Extremely high frequency sound waves

44

drive out rats and mice. Doesn't affect people, cats or dogs. Keeps an indoor area up to 2,000 square feet, rodent free." But where do they go and how often do you use it and won't they just come back when things quiet down? I'd like to talk to someone who has used one, but the subject of rats never seems to come up at dinner parties. Even though D-Con and the feed the rats eat is expensive, we haven't spent *that* kind of money on rats—so far.

Owls and hawks are natural predators and are free, but our rats spend most of their time under the barn. Once in a while, toward dusk, we'll see one pop out from between the rocks of the foundation only to scuttle back. It would take a very attentive hawk on constant duty to catch him. We think our resident owl makes off with the dead ones, which we heave across the road into the woods. We've thrown 218 rats over there, and there isn't a trace of one. In fact they are always gone by morning, which also suggests the nocturnal habits of an owl. A weasel might attack a rat, but we don't want a weasel around the place eyeing our chickens hungrily because they prefer chicken meat and so do we. My father had a pet ferret when he was a boy, and the ferret was expert at diving down a rabbit hole and bringing back a rabbit. A ferret would probably catch rats too, but my books about North American mammals say that ferrets in the wild live in the Midwest between the Mississippi and the Rockies, usually in prairie-dog communities. I wonder how my father got his pet ferret in Tecumseh, Mich. In 1901 a prairie-dog town was described by Vernon Bailey. It was almost continuous for 250 miles and was 100 miles in width; it was estimated that it contained a population of 400,000,000. That's one thousand times the population of cows *and* people in Vermont. "Towns" like that no longer exist. Good thing! Can you imagine a prairie-dog town in Vermont?

Perhaps what we need is a brace of those "attack cats" pictured on posters and T-shirts. The cat we did have flatly refused to be a barn cat. Maybe she knew when she was outnumbered. She much preferred Wolfs to rats, chickens, or pigs, and she was terrified of the geese in our pasture. Actually, she wasn't a very athletic little cat and the food at the house didn't require any effort beyond a wistful look when the refrigerator door was opened.

Of course if our barn were about to collapse the rats would desert it, but that seems even more impractical than shutting the barn door after your horse is stolen. There was a common belief in Ireland that rats could be destroyed by metrical charms. Ben Jonson wrote, "Rhime them to death, as they do the Irish rats." Even though I passed Mt. Holyoke College's versification course, there was no mention of exorcist poetry that I recall. In mythology, Apollo killed rats with arrows, but they were a special kind of far darting arrows available only to the gods. George once shot a snake in our Weston, Mass., garden with a bow and arrow because firearms were forbidden within the town limits, but you've got to be able to see your target before you can shoot at it. I can barely pull the string on our bow, so it would undoubtedly be only the fabled side of the barn door that I'd hit.

There are two suggestions in Sir James Frazer's *Golden Bough* that I like. "In the Ardennes they say that to get rid of rats you should repeat the following words: 'Erat verbum, apud Deum vestrum.' Male and female rats, I conjure you by the great God, to go out of my house, out of all my habitations, and to betake yourselves to such and such a place, there to end your days. 'Decretis, reversis et disembarassis virgo potens, clemens, justitiae.' Then write the same words on

46

pieces of paper, fold them up and place one of them under the door by which the rats are to go forth, and the other on the road which they are to take. This exorcism should be performed at sunrise." Some years ago an American farmer was reported to have written a civil letter to the rats, telling them that his crops were short, that he could not afford to keep them through the winter, that he had been very kind to them, and that for their own good he thought they had better leave him and go to some of his neighbors who had more grain. This document he pinned to a post in his barn for the rats to read.

I'm sure the neighbors would have explicit suggestions for the road *we* should take if we tried this—the interstate highway to the state mental hospital at Waterbury.

My favorite is an ancient Greek treatise on farming with this advice, "Take a piece of paper and write on it as follows, 'I adjure you, ye mice [rats] here present, that ye neither injure me or suffer another mouse [rat] to do so. I give you yonder field [here you specify the field]; but if I ever catch you here again, by the Mother of the Gods I will rend you in seven pieces.' Write this and stick the paper on an unhewn stone in the field before sunrise, taking care to keep the written side up."

That's telling them! You dirty rats!

File under Fiction

Any resemblance between what grows in our garden and what ornaments the pages of the seed catalogs is purely coincidental. If I won't accept blame for the melons that attained only baseball size before the first frost, neither can I take credit for the zucchini crop, which if laid end to end would reach from Jericho to Big Sur and plop into the Pacific. There are times in August when I wish they would. Is there anything more persistent than zucchini? Yes, I know, dandelions, purslane, and milkweed, but in spite of Euell Gibbons's response to the call of the wild garden, my family eyes them with suspicion. The problem is not that the young shoots of any of these aren't as palatable as cultivated greens, but that their timing is off. Fiddleheads in February might look good, but when succulent asparagus, small leaves of Bibb lettuce, and spring onions are beckoning from the garden why revert to the wild?

Back to the seed catalogs. Those perfect crimson satin globes on the cover certainly brighten the coffee table in January, but where are they in July? Just tiny green marbles cowering among the leaves. And after reading the instructions in the Sunday *New York Times* garden section, you carefully nip off most of the side shoots and excess foliage, and what happens? They still just sit there week after week pretending to be peas. How can asparagus stalks grow as much as eight inches in one day while the tomatoes in the next row look the same as they did the day you transplanted them? Worse, in fact. After the tomato plants recover from the shock of transplanting and decide to perk up and look around, you expect a little action. There they are, a foot high with little yellow blossoms full of promise. Within the next week or two half the leaves will also be yellow, the blossoms will have dropped off, and those tiny green tomatoes could still fit into a pea shooter.

That child in the catalog who is standing next to an indoor tomato plant looks familiar. The one-and-one-half-foot plant has twenty brilliant red tomatoes on it and she is holding a big basket simply overflowing with ripe tomatoes, giving the intended impression that she has just picked them from this same plant. You know why this five-year-old looks familiar? She is the same child who can run a rototiller all by herself, and it must be her sister who unfolds a Hide-A-Bed unaided. The name of the tomato plant she is displaying is Pixie, and I'm not surprised. In fact Pixie is an understatement. Houdini would be more appropriate.

New in the 1970s was Burpee's Right Royal Squash. It was pictured with Prince Philip at the Canadian Winter Fair in Toronto, and the Prince is smiling broadly. I know why. The accompanying description also says that the squash weighs more than 300 pounds. "It isn't an eating squash but it is just the thing to raise for exhibition, and the children will love its spectacular size. It needs plenty of room in your garden or you could let it grow across your lawn and watch the neighbors stare!" Anyone willing to devote a suburban garden to a 300 pound squash deserves the stares of the neighbors. This must be the pumpkin shell that Peter put his wife into. Well, he was a pumpkin eater and if he couldn't eat the whole thing what else could he do with it? It certainly would be cheaper than a mental hospital for a wife who would plant such a monstrosity.

Why is it that the pictured cucumbers have no spines, but the ones in our garden are so prickly that I could use my hands for a colander all summer long? It is partly because we grow the pickling rather than the slicing variety, and they usually photograph the smooth, sleek, slicing kinds. George develops strange symptoms if he eats raw cucumbers, but we all consider pickles among the good things in life. Is it true what they say about the Burpless Hybrid? But how will I get George to try them the first time?

There is a picture of a pole lima that grew up a TV antenna, turned around, and came down again and measured thirty feet when it was finally disengaged from the house. It says that people came from all over to see it. Well, I'm not that lonely, and while I am addicted to Kentucky Wonders they do present problems. When we grew them on seven-foot poles they didn't turn around and come back down. They hung off the top in streamers and waved in the breeze like the ribbons on a May pole. The next year George put up eight-foot poles, and the best beans hung in great clusters well out of reach over my head. Anyway, who wants to drag out a ladder and scramble up onto the roof to the TV antenna to get a few handfulls of beans for dinner? No wonder people came from all over to see the fair lady upon a white house picking lima beans. I would have just sat up there and tossed beans down to the curiosity seekers.

If those overdeveloped specimens frighten you, the catalogs suggest midget vegetables. There is a golden midget corn with ears only four inches long and near enough to the ground so that a three-year-old can pick them. You don't have to plant midget varieties for that reason. When Debbie was three she came trotting up from the garden with both small fists full of two-inch ears of golden bantam that she had picked for her dolls. When I consider how I felt about our corn crop, I marvel that Debbie lived to become four. There is a small cabbage that is called Little Leaguer because the heads are softball size. But let's not press our luck with the young. Debbie also had a fondness for digging up the seeds a half-hour after they were planted to see how they were getting along. Both girls were continually under foot during the years when they sat on tomato plants, pulled up carrots to observe their progress, and couldn't tell a bean from a burdock. But just about the time when they were able to distinguish corn from milkweed, their services in the garden could not even be bought. I was astonished to see Patty's picture in a Helsinki newspaper and find out that she was newsworthy because she was planting American vegetables in a garden plot outside of Helsinki. And Debbie and Steve now have a handsome, composted garden with raised beds and herbs that I only see in glass jars in gourmet food shops.

Mature ears of that midget corn would have been nice for the baby raccoons in our garden who found holding the standard-size ear fatiguing. But our garden is not only fenced but electrified. I have some doubt that it is either the fence or the shock that deters them. I think it is the thock-thock-thock sound of the mechanism that makes the masked bandits move on to quieter pastures.

In spite of recurrent crops of rocks and rodents, potato

bugs and cucumber beetles, there is nothing so satisfying as watching your garden grow. Maybe it is because of the multiple obstacles that you feel such pride in the first handful of sugar snap peas. It's not just that they will taste so fresh and crisp and tender. It is that they are a part of such an ever-changing alchemy of growing, blossoming, and fruiting that each day there is something new to harvest. Working in the garden gives me a sense of accomplishment that I've never found on the golf course. It puts you and your current anxieties in sensible perspective. Minor crises shrink as you work your way down the rows with a wide blue sky overhead and the teeming productive soil pressing warm and moist on your knees. If the beans can hunch up through the resistant earth and burst into bloom, the chances are that you can too.

May

Wouldn't it be wonderful if May could last for three months? I could manage very well without November and March if you insist on twelve months.

All through the woods and along the roadsides the shadbushes have foamed into bloom. Sometimes, from a distance, they look misty pink, the color of arbutus, which of course is Mayflower. The illusion of pink shadbush is because the tiny emerging new leaves are deep crimson.

By the first week in May our early daffodils are in full triumphant bloom, the strident King Alfred trumpets, followed by the more modest narcissi and the fragrant daffodils, Suzy and Cheerfulness. During the night of May 6 our ewe dropped a little ewe lamb. The ewe's restless behavior and obvious discomfort told us that she was in labor and after two hours George and I were as uneasy as she was, though we kept a respectful distance. But in the morning Mama was cropping grass as though nothing had happened and wobbling at her side was her beautiful lamb, totally unafraid as I approached. Within a few hours she was trotting around and taking a few experimental leaps in the air, something it takes a human baby a year to accomplish. When she nursed, jabbing at her mother's milk bag with typical fervor, the lamb wiggled her long tail so vigorously that it looked as though it were going in circles.

Our two female African geese appointed themselves guardians and honk and hiss and stretch out their long necks if we approach the lamb. They make it difficult for us to establish any kind of relationship with her. Within a week the lamb became shy of humans, flinched if I touched her, and bounded away. But the ewe became friendlier toward us, allowing us to scratch her neck and trotting over to the fence if I held out a handful of grass.

The greening of Vermont happens in May. Everything is growing at a phenomenal rate, including the lawn grass, unfortunately, but the onion sets, radishes, lettuce, and spinach are an inch high by mid-May and we can eat asparagus every other day. Leaves are bursting out, first the waxy, chartreuse leaves of the "popples," the sugar maples with their new moist leaves that look like half-opened Japanese parasols. In early May the gray birches still are crowned with dark brown twigs, but by the middle of May their tiny new leaves and pendulous catkins look as though a green mist is caught in their crowns. Patches of bluets spread out on the hillside pastures, skim-milk blue. They are called Quaker ladies in some parts of the country, but not in Vermont.

The second half of May is all shades of green, from chartreuse corn and lettuce seedlings to the frosty bluegreen of the pea vines. Our old apple tree is a giant's bouquet of pink and white, and the lilacs at the corner of every farmhouse are the deep purple of the tight buds before they open out into lavender flowers.

In mid-May we added a gander to our two geese, and his behavior outdid Bobby Riggs' male chauvinism. He spread his huge wings, thrust out his long neck, and squawked, strutted, and charged at the two females, ordering them around and driving them in front of him. He was so obnoxious that I felt embarassed for him. He never actually attacked us, but he squonked and raced toward us threateningly, stopping just short of contact. He also nipped and chased the ewe, driving her away from the feeding pan, so we gave them another pan. Oddly enough, he didn't attack the lamb, although as she grew bigger he would threaten and chase her. She seemed to tease him, trotting up close, retreating when he hissed and stuck out his neck, but then going right back up to him. Perhaps she was trying to get him to play with her. She would leap and gambol in front of her mother, inviting her to join the dance and then go and do the same thing with the gander, to no avail. Grown-ups are so stuffy!

On May 19 we drove over to Huntington to get two six-week-old piglets. A piglet in a grain bag is an undulating, grunting mound bumping all over the back of the truck. I'm always afraid they'll get out or suffocate. They never do either. But they are funny and shy when first put into their pen, dashing for the far corner, facing the wall, motionless except for their twitching tails. Pigs are fun and their total dedication is an inspiration. Of course it is solely directed toward eating, but their enthusiasm enhances the pleasure of feeding them.

In the last week of May 1980 our daughter Patty, who lives in Finland, came with her two little boys for a long visit. Peter was almost two and Patrick just four. Peter is solid and chubby with almost white hair and a wide, disarming smile. Patrick is slender, quicksilver in motion with golden blond hair, not nearly so shy as last year, and speaking beautiful English as well as Finnish and some Swedish. On the very last day of May, 1981, Debbie and Steve's baby, Morgan Wolf Page, was born. Three little grandsons, two piglets, a little lamb, and fluffy goslings, all vocal, all as fresh and young as May.

The Year of Seven Springs

There is nothing unique in choosing spring for my favorite season. Practically everyone else in the world who lives in a multiseason climate feels the same way. But perhaps the long wait for it in Vermont sharpens the yearning for the first glimpse of green. Spring after summer might be a pale performance, but spring after five months of snow and another six weeks of mud is so exalting that it evokes some sort of responsive action. I am compelled to poke among the dead leaves hunting for the first spikes of tulips and daffodils. I straighten bureau drawers and gather up a load to go to the cleaners. All the way there I look in every yard for crocuses and snowdrops. From pussy-willows to peonies I am grateful to be alive and in reasonably acute possession of my senses.

One memorable spring we moved from Ardsley, N. Y., to Vermont in May, which gave us a repeat performance of tulips, apple blossoms, and lilacs. Another time we had a double helping of blossoming when we moved from Weston, Mass. to Vermont in the last week of May.

But the spring after we returned to Vermont we decided we really must go to visit Patty in Finland, a country that was rapidly becoming her natural habitat. And once the tickets were bought, there was no reason for not stopping in several other countries going and coming. George wanted me to see Zurich, Copenhagen, Stockholm, and Lund. I wanted to go to London to visit Elsie and Ralph Barton, who took Patty in when she was desperately sick with hepatitis in 1967 and cared for her a whole month until she was well enough to return home.

When we left Vermont on May 4, there were still several feet of skiable snow on the mountain and a few inches of it cringing on the north side of the house where anemic-looking spears of daffodils were poking through in search of the sun. So we were amazed and delighted, as we came in for a landing at Zurich, to see that the tall red-tiled roofs and Lombardy poplars were surrounded by horse chestnut trees in blossom. Trees were in full leaf. The parks were ablaze with solid beds of scarlet and gold tulips, great round beds of purple velvet pansies with not one petal of another color, and on either side other circular beds with borders of brilliant blue forget-me-nots framing masses of rose-colored Darwin tulips. Out in the countryside on the way to Lucerne, each chalet had a neat little garden with rows of tulips, lettuces, and onions being softly snowed upon by falling cherry blossoms. I had been almost afraid to return to Grindelwald because I had spent the month of May there when I was eight years old and was afraid that tourism and skiing might have spoiled the sight and sound of spring that I remembered so clearly. But of course the mountains were still magnificently impregnable, and the main street of the village, though it had acquired souvenir shops, espresso stands, and the more aggressive look of prosperity, was still so dominated by the enormity and closeness of the Eiger and its glacier that any discordant note was as unobtrusive as the call of a kingfisher just above Niagara Falls.

The pension where I had stayed with my grandparents, sister, and mother, the Schönegg, was now the Schönegg Motor Hotel, but it was still in the same spot on the side of the hill. The tiny chapel at the end of the street wore another half-century more lightly than I; in the little cemetery in the churchyard every grave wore a coverlet of flowers, not just a wreath or bouquet withering at the headstone but the entire rectangle of each grave was planted solidly with primulas, pansies, tulips, forget-me-nots, and even, most exciting of all, one or two honest-to-goodness Alpine blue gentians! What a lovely idea as a symbol of resurrection, to make each grave into a beautiful flower bed in that tiny walled churchyard. And how dramatic the brilliant colors were against the polished black headstones.

From Switzerland we flew to Stockholm and found that the calendar had slipped back a few notches. Daffodils were just unfolding. The new waxy leaves on the trees were just crowding into a shade, and all the benches in the parks were turned toward the sun and filled with people of all ages, their eyes closed and their faces upturned basking in the light and welcoming the return of spring.

In Helsinki when we saw Patty's tiny figure on the observation deck of the airport silhouetted against the pale blue Finnish sky, we realized that spring was only just beginning in Finland. The Finns have a special word for this season. They say the birch trees are in "mouse ears" and branches with these tiny delicate leaves are sold in the markets along with flowers and the birch twigs that are used in the saunas. Flowers are very important in the daily lives of the people of Helsinki. They have a lovely custom of taking just a few, perhaps three, sprays of fragrant freesia in different colors or one rose and a few forget-me-nots to their hostess when they are invited to her home. The ladies in the florist shops are very helpful and gracious about trying different combinations. There is no feeling that they expect you to buy a dozen roses or a fifteen-dollar azalea plant. Everyone buys flowers or leaves. They are not considered a luxury, and there were a few fresh flowers in every Finnish apartment we visited. The flower market at the harbor was the same cacophony of shouting color that you find in Finnish fabrics. Of course at the time we were there the flowers were either imported or grown in the many greenhouses outside of Helsinki, but before we left a week later, plants in full bloom—hyacinths, tulips, crocuses, and skyblue hydrangeas—were being set out in the parks. There was a huge bowl of butterflylike lilies that almost looked like orchids on a table in our hotel. When I asked the receptionist the name of them, she immediately sent half of them to our room. In the countryside the pine and white birch woods were carpeted with wild flowers, white anemones, and a similar deep blue flower but with different leaves that was unfamiliar to me.

Then we went to Copenhagen, just when the tulip gardens in the Tivoli were at their brightest and perkiest. Each bed separated by color and variety was more splendid than the next—tall, deep red Darwins; exotic-looking parrot tulips; cool white alabaster cups balanced on long delicate stems with wistaria in bloom overhead echoing in color the soft splashing of the fountains. It was mid-spring in Denmark as it had been in Zurich and very much the same when we crossed into southern Sweden and drove through the checkerboard of golden yellow fields of mustard alternating with chocolate brown newly ploughed fields and brilliant green pastures. Lilacs and apple blossoms in Lund, and a nightingale sings in the treetops

59

over a 300-year-old farmhouse where we had dinner in the seacoast village of Falsterbo.

I thought my eyes had been filled with enough flowers to last me through all the winters the rest of my life, but we were unprepared for a beautiful English country estate on display near Hayward's Heath. It was open to the public, but there was not a tourist in sight except us. The visitors were all local English families who each year make a pilgrimage to these azalea and rhododendron gardens and pay a small fee for the benefit of a local charity. The grounds covered acres of lawns and paths that wound under sheltering old beech and oak trees, with, at every turn, a new mass of crimson or pale pink rhododendrons, enormous groupings as big as a house that were set off by the dark green of yew and ivy. Cascades of wistaria and clematis spilled down over the walls of the Tudor mansion. Even the vegetable gardens with the blue green of peas and cabbages and the yellow green of lettuce were as advanced in late May as our garden is in the first week of July. English gardens are comfortable and relaxed, a sweet disorder of colors and fragrances to be enjoyed as much as admired.

It was hard to leave the wonderfully green English countryside to return to I-wasn't-sure-what in Vermont. We had been gone three weeks, and I was afraid that we might have missed our lilacs and apple blossoms. But luck was with us. Spring came late to Vermont that year. Our lilacs were deep purple, just opening, and humming with bees, and the apple trees were only in bud. So we came home to a seventh spring in one season, and after 10,000 miles and no language problem in understanding flowers in five countries the best welcome was to find a bluebird perched in our old reclining apple tree.

It's Not Only Caffein
I Can Do Without

If austerity is to be part of our future way of life there are a few intrusions upon my environment that I not only would not miss, I would happily discard them with the old year. I do not need all those little subscription and discount offers that fall out of magazines and sail across the room to hide out of reach under the table. If they are fastened in they make bulky spots in the magazines so that turning the pages without losing your place becomes difficult. One I could use as a bookmark but I just shook or pulled five out of *Time* and three from *The New Yorker*. If we receive *Time* fifty-two times a year, we don't need to be reminded to renew our subscription 260 times, even if they do offer a reduced rate with a gift subscription to a friend, that is, someone who has a high tolerance for airborne leaflets.

The deluge of unrequested medical magazines is worse. My husband subscribes to three, but twenty fat, slick, heavy, unsolicited periodicals clog our mailbox each week, burden our mail carrier, and contribute to the spiraling cost of postage. Because these are subsidized by the drug companies and sent free to anyone with an M. D. after his name, they are full of ads for the products of those drug companies. I could avert my glance from the full color photographs of malignant tumors or the miserable expression on the faces of depressed patients, but if, by some chance, you should want to read one of the articles, you find it is continued on page 117. Now try to find page 117! Aware that half the magazine is made up of un-numbered pages of advertizing, you guess at where 117 might be. When you can find a numbered page it is 93 or 198 and very soon it isn't only the pages that begin to flip. Some of the women's magazines are fattened with full page ads too, but at least they allow, but do not print, a number for each ad page. So if you come to the bottom of 38 and it is followed by four pages of ads, you know that you'll find your story on page 42 after you have turned two pages. Why can't they put all the ads at the beginning and the end the way the *National Geographic* does? Because the Madison Avenue men want to catch your attention as you frantically hunt for the continu-ation of your story. The more prolonged the search the more opportunities you have to come upon their ad again and again and again till you know the message by heart.

Now if we are really concerned with economy why do the companies of which I am a modest stockholder feel the need to send me big, beautiful, glossy annual reports printed on expensive paper and weighing almost a pound in addition to the usual dreary round of quarterly reports, notices, and proxies? Do they fantasize that because I glance briefly at the colored pictures that I actually read all those figures? No doubt they are required by law to keep me advised of their financial condition, but if they think that the deluxe appear-ance of the annual report impresses this stockholder, they are wrong. All it does is impress me with the fact that they certain-ly are throwing around a lot of money, including mine. I'd welcome a mimeographed sheet with a note to the effect that by economizing on their annual report they have been able to increase our dividends.

We have a lot to learn from the Europeans. Why don't we walk or bicycle more often instead of wasting gasoline riding to the butcher, the baker, and the candlestickmaker and then making a big production out of jogging several miles a day for exercise? Why don't we carry string bags to the supermarket instead of chopping down trees to make paper bags that are buried at the sanitary landfill because the stores will not take them back to use again? If one of the supermarkets announced that they were discontinuing horse racing games, green stamps, lucky numbers and instead were reducing their prices, they'd be mobbed with customers. When peanut butter became an endangered spread and the few remaining jars were doubled in price it was blamed on a poor peanut crop. But when an abundance of peanut butter reappeared on the shelves a few months later why did the price stay up at the level it had reached when it was scarce? And how did that peanut crop mature so quickly? We tried to grow peanuts once and they take forever, or more specifically between four and five months to mature. I admit that it wasn't very bright to try to grow peanuts in Vermont or anything else that needs a long hot summer when our capricious growing season is only that long about once in three years. We tried it for fun just to see nuts growing underground like potatoes. All we saw were tiny inedible embryos that never reached the size or shape of a peanut.

But before we get out of the supermarket let me suggest that when we are trying to conserve energy, why are the stores kept so cold in the summer that you turn blue in the frozen food section? I could do without the deep freeze. We get enough cold in the winter to last me all year. And I don't need music to push my cart by unless I get one of those recalcitrant carts whose left front wheel marches to a different drummer.

I applaud unit pricing because I defy anyone to compare the prices of three-ounce and eight-ounce containers without a calculator. But when I see price stickers three deep on a commonly used item I don't see how the personnel has time to reprice the stock so often. No wonder there is such a long wait for the two check-out counters in operation. All the other checkers are racing up and down the aisles repricing everything.

Most of all we could do without the notion that bigger is better. In New York City recently I saw one big black hearse-size limousine after another. The single passenger needed an intercom to communicate with the driver. And this in a city where traffic is so jammed up that it takes three-quarters of an hour to get across town. In motels where lamps and pictures are enormous to discourage you from taking them home, why is it necessary to put paper bags over the drinking glasses and paper barriers across the toilet seats? It doesn't prove that either are sterile but just that someone, eventually you, is paying for this wastepaper cover-up.

I could do without menus the size of the Magna Charta, pepper grinders as tall as baseball bats, which only the waiter is allowed to handle, pocketbooks that could double as over-night bags, and down-filled coats that make you look like that fat man made out of rubber tubes who used to advertize tires. I don't need the gargantuan imitation pewter service plates whose only function is to exercise the waiter. Foil wrapping on baked potatoes only steams the potatoes, and an occasional scrap of foil hides in a bite of potato and sets your teeth on edge.

The truth is that we could dine on smoked salmon, beef Wellington, and cherries jubilee at home for half the cost of the chicken Kiev whose bill is so discreetly presented face down on a silver salver.

I could do without that, too.

June

May is full of budding and early blossoming, promises and expectations. June is fulfillment of May's promise, lush and green. Amy Hunt's old-fashioned garden is a solid mass of bloom, day lilies, phlox, daffodils, peonies, and lupine, no vacant spots, no visible weeds, just a blanket of variegated pastels. I almost drive off the road admiring it as I go to the village.

The birds are nesting, and a robin pair scolds me when I walk near the spring on the way to the brook. For days I looked up into the pine branches hoping to see the nest. I was looking too far away and too high. It was right over my head. The babies left the nest in mid-June. There has been no evidence of a second family in that nest. Maybe Mrs. Robin decided the spot was too public and will rear her second family farther from the path. Robins are not usually shy. They fuss when you come near but usually build their nest not far from a house.

The female geese are setting again, and this time we are not disturbing the eggs. Now that we have a gander we are hoping for goslings. But are these eggs, laid the week after the gander joined us, fertile? Thirty days is a long time for Patrick and Peter to wait. It's a long time for me too and think how long it must seem to the two geese who almost never leave the nest! When do they eat and drink? Geese normally drink a great deal of water but only very rarely do we see either one leave her nest now. Such a bleak-looking nest, a few sticks on the bare ground. No wonder they don't dare leave them. The unguarded eggs would not only be vulnerable to attacks from predators but could be trampled by the clumsy big-footed gander or our two sheep. In the second week we got one peek at the nests. One nest that had had two eggs in it was empty, but there were only a few tiny shell fragments. Who stole them or ate them or both? A goose egg is very big and heavy. Could a raccoon or fox carry it or even break that hard shell? I had to whang the goose eggs hard on the kitchen counter to break the thick, stonelike shell when we were eating the goose eggs earlier in the spring. The other nest that had had three eggs in it had only one egg. Our hopes for goslings were diminishing. But on June 25, as I walked to the garden and glanced over at the geese, there was a ball of yellow and beige fluff waddling along on outsize orange feet between the two geese. He was so funny and cute I laughed out loud and could hardly wait for Moutsie (Patrick) and Petsku (Peter) to come over to see him. They were delighted with him and hunkered down on their little heels to be nearer his level, making little "Ah-ah" sounds at him. He was named Bruce goose.

Babies are now everywhere! Two little blond grandsons, two pink piglets in the barn, Bruce goose, and two kittens, one golden and the other pale pink-beige, the color of pink mink. These kittens slept on the porch deck. One morning the pink mink was there. No trace of the golden one. Could our resident owl who makes off with the rats we catch in the traps in the barn have gotten it? We had heard a squawk in the night and feared the worst. We hoped it had just gone on an "expedition," but it never returned.

Peas are now in bloom, delicate white blossoms among the pewter blue green vines and leaves. Patty and I have been picking strawberries at a nearby farm. She and I are the two in the family with the berry-picking syndrome. We creep along the rows, smelling the fragrant berries, the sun warm on our backs. Even when we have picked all we need for jam, freezing, and eating fresh, it is very hard to stop. Surely the next plant will have especially juicy berries. The small strawberry patch in our own garden had lots of berries but something ate most of them. I had put a net over them so it couldn't have been birds, and it was pretty dry for slugs. Could it have been red squirrels or chipmunks?

We've been eating asparagus all month. An asparagus bed is a real delight once you get it going and relatively weed-free. Having been accustomed to the fat, white, European blanched asparagus, our Finnish son-in-law viewed our green, amethyst-tipped spears with some misgivings at first but he has been converted.

Not all of June is idyllic, however. Just to keep our feet on the ground the potato bugs, slow-moving, dumb bugs appear. They are easy to spot because of their red color and not too revolting to handpick and crush if you are wearing heavy boots—and the black flies that I never see until it is too late.

June used to be the traditional time for graduations and weddings. Now graduations are often in May and weddings may be anytime or any place. George and I were exploring Mt. Philo and a group of young people were assembling on the summit for a wedding. But it is a happy time, a time of wrapping up a segment of education or life. This is the summer that Moutsie dared feed the animals except if the pigs jump up or the chickens flapped. And he can almost swim. Petsku is talking more each day and announces "All empty!" when I finish reading him a book. When he emerges from his nap all tousled and pink and eager for whatever the rest of the day holds, he epitomizes the essence of June, fresh and growing and full of life.

Whose Garden Is This, Anyway?

Gardening in Vermont is a form of masochism to which only the true addict would subject himself year after year. Its habituation is supported seasonally, first by the mesmerizing effect of reading and believing seed catalogs in January, and then sustained by anticipation during the horticulturally inactive months of February and March. Then comes the urge to start seeds indoors, appropriately enough on April Fool's day, which presages outdoor planting. In defiance of snow, sleet, and hail, from mid-April, the addict will try to poke such hardies as peas, spinach, lettuce, and radishes into the chilly earth until Memorial Day, when every true Vermonter divides his day between local parade and planting all the rest of his garden.

For the first two weeks in June his disease is often in remission. He may hang up his hoe, answer when spoken to, and resume normal relationships with his family. But during this withdrawal period the gardener is subject to attacks of paranoia. The sentinel crow on a dead elm becomes the incarnation of evil plotting to uproot his corn. He is sure that cutworms are about to garrote the tomato plants, and the most innocent

69

white butterfly is the progenitor of the ubiquitous green cabbage worm. A host of larger if less visible predators—woodchucks, deer, and finally, when the corn is just ripe, raccoons—are already inviting their relatives to dine on the fruits of his labors.

We've been under the influence of gardening for thirty-two years. Or I should say I have. My husband is a social gardener who can take it or leave it. He does the heavy work like rototilling, spreading manure and lime, putting up fences, and setting up the Hav-a-Hart trap, but he doesn't bring the garden home at night the way I do. I think our four-footed predators know that the two-legged animal with blond hair, who talks to herself, does not know how to load a gun and refuses to set a leg trap.

You would think that three decades of reading and weeding and the expenditure of dried blood, sweat, and tears would lead to expertise. Like bringing up your children, who turn into attractive and capable adults more in spite of your efforts than because of them, success in the garden depends almost as much on environmental factors as on your personal input.

If the last frost is mercifully early and if you have plenty of warmth and moisture for germination followed by enough but not too much rain, and if the insect population is minimal and the furry friends feed outside the fence, you are well on your way to a bountiful harvest. Of course, like raising your children, you do have a certain amount of control over the environment. You can't control the weather except to rush to the garden and cover up tender crops if frost threatens, or splash them with cold water before the sun strikes the frosted plants you forgot to cover up. But you can mulch and weed and plant marigolds and garlic for therapeutic purposes, and dust the cabbage family with Rotenone. Our experience has given us a certain amount of confidence in those areas. But our war with the beasts of the fields is never cold, albeit intermittent. We fenced the garden long ago. After a woodchuck dug an entrance under the fence, we added chicken wire around the bottom of the fence bent outwards into the grass about nine inches. We also set the Hav-a-Hart trap and then did not have a heart when it captured woodchucks and raccoons. By now our garden is the unmarked graveyard for at least a dozen of them. We have tried growing pumpkins in the corn patch, red pepper on corn silk, and dried blood around everything with such varying results that I think the whim of the animal is the determining factor. Finally, George ran an electric wire a few inches above the fence activated by a battery for the few weeks of the corn season. That seems to be the most effective deterrent to raccoons.

Last year we had no animal problems at all, no woodchucks under and no raccoons over the fence. Then this year when the corn was about eight inches high someone broke off and chewed several stalks. The small bean plants next to them were untouched. Our woodchucks are notably fond of young beans. It was too early for raccoons. Was it mice or red squirrels? We never found out, but after I wrapped a few cornstalks in newspapers it didn't happen again. Maybe we are not the only ones turned off by the news.

That was early June and all went well until mid-August, when the hearts were eaten out of some broccoli and Brussels-sprout plants. Normally, we would suspect a woodchuck and so George and I crept around the periphery of the garden on our hands and knees hunting for a telltale hole, to the bewilderment of a passerby. We fenced over one shallow spot where someone had been digging, but the next morning the tendrils of the tall Alderman peas had been nipped off at eye level. Jerusalem artichokes were missing some leaves at the same height. Now my eye level is more than five feet off the ground, and no woodchuck can reach that high even on his tiptoes. That could only have been done by a deer. We have never had a deer in the garden, though we have once or twice seen one on our land. So George hung aluminum disks, and I ringed the garden with dried blood and covered the remaining members of the cabbage family with netting. I even suggested to George that I had read that human urine around the garden was said to be a deer deterrent and that he was better equipped anatomically than I to provide that service. He was not fascinated and voiced his unwillingness to cooperate in a loud negative monosyllable. Because our garden is visible from the road I found myself reluctant to substitute for him. The most recent suggestion from Stuart Hall, our TV meteorologist, is to walk barefoot around your garden leaving the human scent, which is abhorrent to most wildlife. I haven't tried that for two reasons—my feet. The meadow next to our garden is full of thistles. I may be a masochist but not to the point of baring my soles.

If feet are good, why wouldn't heads be better? I asked Pam Tatro, manager of O'Brien's Beauty Salon in Essex Junction what they do with the locks that are shorn daily. She looked at me oddly but said that they were just thrown away. So I left the beauty parlor clutching a paper bag of hair clippings and scattered the black, auburn, and blond ringlets around the garden.

The next morning I rushed down hoping that there would be no signs of breaking and entering during the night. The deer or woodchuck not only had been in the garden overnight, he had chewed up a whole cabbage into juicy coleslaw right through the netting and finished off a row of beans. I hope the netting caught in his teeth.

Well, back to square one, which I've apparently been trying to pound into the round holes in my head. Didn't I tell you that vegetable gardeners are masochists? But they are also die-hards. I had planted so many succession crops of beans that we've had all we can eat and some to process in spite of the depredations. Fortunately our night feeder prefers the leaves while we favor the beans. Our corn is unscathed so far, but my bare legs are scathed daily while I thrash through the jungle of prickly pumpkin vines to test the ears for ripeness.

We are only a step away from search lights and transistor radios or maybe the burglar alarm system that we have reluctantly installed in our house. But one of the benefits of the garden is supposed to be economy. As it is, we could buy more corn than we can eat in one season for less than the cost of the battery we use for one month. But that isn't the point. I love the garden. It's my psychiatrist and my health spa. It is an ever-changing daily miracle, and perhaps pitting your wits against those of the four-legged predators is part of the excitement. Even if they ate half the produce, the half they allowed us to harvest is worth all the anguish. Anyone who has ever tasted new peas, corn, broccoli, and sun-warmed tomatoes fresh from the garden knows that you can't stop after the first bite. It's a life-long addiction and while, unlike the usual addict, I admit it freely, I really have not the slightest desire for a cure.

Happy as a Clam

What's so happy about a clam? I haven't seen any evidence of euphoria or depression in the clams of my acquaintance. But they do have one advantage over humans. They can and do shut out their environment by a flick of a muscle or retreat into the sand at a speed frustrating to the amateur clam digger. A turtle also can withdraw beneath his shell and protect his vulnerable parts under his rock-hard carapace.

Humans throughout history have put on shells of armor and coats of mail or, more recently, football and motorcycle helmets and wet suits to protect their fragile bodies. But there are times when the desire to withdraw is not so much to save our skins as our psyches. We are so hell-bent for togetherness that we neglect the need for aloneness, which has nothing to do with loneliness.

Last winter when George was suddenly threatened by blindness in one eye and had to undergo a long operation followed by double patches and uncertain results, we both were surprised to find that we had a great desire to be by ourselves, to be alone together. I suppose you could call that licking your wounds, but don't forget that wound licking originated as a therapeutic measure. As the prognosis improved and George was able to resume his usual activities, our clam shell opened automatically and once again we became interested in the sea around us.

There are other kinds of "alone" situations where the clam shell has dual occupancy. A couple in love often feel that the rest of the world is too much with them. They are self-sufficient and resent intrusion upon their privacy.

Living in the country we are well aware of the mare-and-colt, ewe-lamb, cat-and-kittens bond that keeps the rest of the world at a respectful distance from each of these units. From the viewpoint of a grandmother I've seen my daughters hole up emotionally with their newborn babies. I did it too when they were babies, but of course at that time I was inside the clam shell. It is not learned. It is instinctive and probably triggered by hormonal changes. It also is baffling to most new fathers. His feelings are ambivalent. He can understand the phenomenon intellectually but can't really accept it emotionally. His previously attentive wife has temporarily taken the receiver to his direct line off the hook and she is tuned out, in a little cocoon of motherhood. She can't help it. She is biologically programmed that way, and it is another form of clam shell that will open in time.

Almost every hospital patient knows how fatiguing visitors are. It is great to see them but if they stay more than five minutes and begin to talk about their lives, the poor patient who is a cross between a captive audience and a sitting duck, begins to develop predictable symptoms—sweating palms and feet, rapid pulse, and exhaustion. The female patient may cry when her visitors leave. The male will get crabby. Both have lost control of their environment and the ability to escape—clams on the half shell.

I have trouble empathizing with those who have a fear of being alone. Granting that eating alone in a restaurant, for a woman, or coping with unfamiliar currency or inadequate language skill in a foreign country are forms of loneliness that I can do without, I still need and enjoy long stretches of being alone. Gardening is wonderfully relaxing and restorative for that reason, just you and a soft breeze, an inquisitive robin, and a small brown toad, sociability enough on a warm June day to recharge your batteries and restore your equanimity.

So maybe clams are happy after all and we all need to withdraw to muster strength for the next project. Robert Frost, alone in his woods cutting his winter supply of fuel said,

> I see for Nature no defeat
> In one tree's overthrow
> Or for myself in my retreat
> For yet another blow.

July

July used to be firecrackers and sparklers, peas and salmon, the "glorious Fourth," which I dreaded as a child because I hated the noise of the giant firecrackers and those miserable torpedos that the boys hurled down on the sidewalk. Now in Vermont the 4th is quiet until evening, when there are several large fireworks displays over Lake Champlain and the Vermont Symphony plays, at Shelburne Farms, the 1812 Overture, complete with canon.

Our peas don't quite make it by the 4th of July. In fact, we ate the first not-quite-ripe ones on the 11th so that Patty and Tage could have a memory of ambrosia to take back to Finland with them the next day. The little boys wouldn't eat them anyway. Their notion of food for the gods is anything under the golden arches of "NuckDonald's," where they chomp blissfully on "fench fies" and the contents of a hamburger roll. They consider the roll just a handy container. Even Petsku, who approaches food with the enthusiasm of a baby robin, doesn't care much for vegetables. He likes potatos and the "wallow ones" (carrots) but so far hasn't developed his mother's green tongue.

Clumps of tawny wood lilies now enliven every roadside. When we transplanted some to a flower bed, they didn't bloom the first year but this year the blossom stalks shot way up above the lemon day lilies and they look angular like gawky boys wearing last year's outgrown pants. Along the roadside they never seem gawky.

Long dry spells in July make everyone twitchy about water. Is there enough for our neighbor's cows? Will the peas yellow before we've had a good crop? Should we use the washing machine or take a load to the laundromat? The pool below the waterfall becomes our bathtub as well as a recreational swimming pool, and the little boys take to the woods instead of the bathroom.

But water isn't the only worry in the garden. We had dug up some Jerusalem artichokes and planted them outside the garden because of their aggressive fecundity in the vegetable garden. But something has been nibbling the leaves at night, high up, at eye level. It must be a deer. The leaves of the horseradish have also been eaten. It is no great loss outside the garden, but we do have a new mystery predator inside the fence. When the cornstalks were less than a foot high two of them were chewed off six inches above the ground. The next night, two more. There was no evidence that a woodchuck had dug under the fence, and whenever a woodchuck has invaded our garden in the past he has never been satisfied with a few bites. He would mow down a whole row of beans in one night.

Part of the excitement of a garden is that something new happens every day, or night, and the way a garden grows is different each year. This year our spinach, beets, and carrots are beautiful. Last year I had to replant beets and cucumbers. Last year the zucchini was early and plentiful. This year there are only a few tiny ones by the last week in July, two weeks late.

This year we planted early and late peas, and the late ones, Alderman, are so prolific and long-bearing that I'm going to plant more of them next year. Also, they are much easier to pick. They grow as tall as six feet so you can just walk along and pick them instead of creeping along on your knees or bent double poking through the vines hunting for the Blue Bantams. Besides, the dwarf varieties aren't really dwarf. They all need support in spite of the promises of the seed catalogs. And the dwarf horticultural beans insinuate themselves far beyond their appointed rows.

The baby goose, Bruce, uses the sheep and geese's water pan as a swimming pool and paddles around happily while his parents dip their bills in his wake. He ducks and preens his fluff with vigor, almost capsizing his buoyant little body.

Broccoli is heading up, and miraculously we have no cabbage worms this year, so far. No cucumber beetles either. In fact, this is the most bug-free year we've had in a long time.

In the last week of July the zucchinis are growing several inches a day. Zucchini soup base (zucchinis, onions, and chicken stock all cooked together and then whirled in the blender) freezes well. And a zucchini casserole (cheese, onions, bread crumbs, and cubed zucchini) tastes fine in January even if it isn't quite the same tender-crisp bright green product that it is fresh in July. Zucchini rounds replace crackers as carriers for cheese or dips with drinks during their seasonal overabundance, and slivers of zucchini find their way into tossed salads and substitute for noodles in lasagna, providing you parboil and drain them well first.

If only everything in the garden was as continuously fruitful as zucchini! Four plants of butterbush winter squash produce 12 squash. Four plants of zucchini probably produce 200. For over two months our cupboard is never bare of the slender green phalanxes. Zucchini would be a good symbol for July—green, fast-growing, and burgeoning with life.

The Sibilance of Summer

Summer is a soft word, and many of the sounds of summer fall gently on the ear, evoking images that reach back to childhood memories. The plinking of new peas in a saucepan, the taffeta rustle of corn leaves in the breeze, the plop of a strawberry pulled from the plant, the distant clacking of a combine, the clatter and creak of horses hooves and wagon wheels as a hay wagon lumbers up into the barn, the hum of bees in the garden while picking beans, the imperious crow of the bantam rooster down the road.

There is the muttering of distant thunder and the sharp staccato notes of the first raindrops as the storm gathers momentum. Birdsong is quieter in summer than in the spring. Territorial proclamations and courting melodies have been diminished by the demands of nesting and the interminable stuffing of the young. But the robins herald the rain, and the catbird's impersonations lure you onto the porch to see if one bird can really make all that music.

And when the storm has passed down the valley and a fresh cool breeze stirs the dripping evergreens, the wistful notes of the hermit thrush also drop like liquid in the forest, where the horizontal rays of the setting sun slant through the heavy branches.

So many of the country summer sounds, from the tentative notes of "Taps" on Memorial Day to the rumble of the resumed rounds of the yellow school buses on the Wednesday after Labor Day, are the sounds of gathering and harvesting what has grown on the land. They are reassuring sounds reminding us that our fundamental strength and satisfaction comes from the earth.

August

August is the ripe month. Everything in the garden matures at a rate that keeps you running from garden to sink to stove, pickling, canning, freezing. The kitchen has a wonderful smell of vinegar, onions, cucumbers, and spices when the bread-and-butter pickles are simmering. And what is more satisfying than rows of jellies and pickles? The freezer contents aren't that visible, but they add to the sense of being partly self-sufficient.

Goldenrod is everywhere. Funny how one flower will dominate a season. In late May there is a lilac bush in every yard that is ignored except when it is a mass of fragrant blossoms. It is like learning a new word that then pops up frequently. Milkweed pods are plumping out. I often pick some for Dorcas Houston to freeze. I have never tried them, but they are said to be like okra. I am not afraid of wildlings. I love the dandelion rosettes for salad, and we also use strawberry leaves and violet leaves, both loaded with Vitamin C. But just at the time that the milkweed pods are an inch long and ready to eat, so is everything else—beans, zucchini, the last of the peas, and the first of the corn. You're not going to convince me that milkweed pods are better than those. Our corn is late this year.

It usually matures two weeks after Burpee's expected date. This year it was more than three weeks after the catalog date. Tomatoes expected August 10 were edible September 1.

The roadside wildflowers are at their best—chicory, Queen Anne's lace, black-eyed Susans, and goldenrod. Chicory is summer's blue flower in Vermont. The tiny shy bluets wash over our hillsides in the spring, sky-blue chicory is rampant along the roadsides in summer, and then suddenly in fall it is lavender-blue asters that are everywhere. Summer guests return from a walk in August bearing a bunch of wildflowers, and they always have one small mystery flower, never the same one and always difficult to identify.

The summer guests are almost as abundant as the wildflowers. It's an easy time to have company because the bounty in the garden makes even the unexpected guest welcome. If you have platters of corn, bowls of beans, zucchini casseroles, and blueberry pie no one notices that the roast, which is stretching to serve four, was only meant for two. In fact, we've noticed that our own appetite for meat diminishes when we have a variety of fresh vegetables. The meat from one pork chop stir-fried with onions, celery, zucchini, and broccoli serves two abundantly.

Bruce goose is now an adolescent, gawky, long in the neck and feet, almost full grown. He may be Brucella instead of Bruce. She (?) does not have the thicker neck and heavy head of a gander. All our creatures are growing up. The lamb has lost her baby voice and playful behavior. She's just another dirty ewe, a clone of her mother. Even when they are put in a fresh pasture, our sheep are convinced that the only edible grass is outside the fence and they nearly strangle themselves pushing through it. The grass just outside the fence is always mowed bald while there is plenty of lush green grass right underfoot. The pigs are two-thirds grown, overstuffed, sleek, and dedicated to the proposition that all men are created equally able to feed pigs day and night.

On hot days the pool is a delight, refreshing but sun-warmed enough to take out the sting. Evenings are cooler now, and the nights are crisp. Shooting stars can be seen on August nights if you can keep your head tilted back for half an hour without inducing a stiff neck. Northern lights pulse across the sky, white and pale green, like wispy clouds being swept across an indigo sky.

I hate to let go of August, and summer. I used to feel that way because it was the end of vacation and the beginning of school, more to be dreaded when I was a teacher than when I was a student. Now it is the realization that the garden will soon be blackened by frost, our pool will go into hibernation with only a black eye open under its lid of ice, and after our vibrant fall we will dig in for the long winter.

You with the Cloven Adidas, Out of the Plastic Pool

We've always been a bit smug about the minimal upkeep of our natural swimming pool. Of course, after a heavy rain it may be roily or "look like beer" as our girls used to say. And I could do without the occasional leech or sharp stone. But it requires no chlorination, no filtering or vacuuming, and the water flows in and out, courtesy of Mill Brook, with no aiding and abetting from us whatsoever.

So when we listen to the tribulations that our friends endure with their expensive, man-made pools, we become positively fatuous.

Our nearest (one-half mile) neighbors, Joan and Jack Cross, have a beautiful pool, sparkling turquoise, surrounded by lawns and flower beds. But one spring when the man came to remove their pool cover, he absent mindedly dumped all the dead and rotten leaves that had accumulated during the winter on the cover not into the nearby woods as directed, but into the pool. Ten days of vacuuming and torrents of colorful language from Jack later, the murky mess had finally filtered itself clean and you could once again see bottom.

The first of our friends to become pool-addicted was Sam

Rowley, who built an outdoor pool in his backyard in West Hartford, Conn., in the 1950s. That was such a success that he built an addition to their house and put in an indoor pool, with gothic windows, plants, and poolside furniture. The only problem, in addition to the initial cost of construction and continuing costs of heating, ventilating, and chlorination, was that the humidity from the pool began to mold and rot the furniture and books in the adjoining rooms of the house. Now the Rowleys live in northern Florida on Jane's great-grand-father's plantation on the St. John's River. There is a lovely walled-in pool fragrant with flowering vines and flowers that are planted inside as well as outside the walls around the pool. We don't have any heavy scented, semi-tropical plants down at our waterfall and pool, but neither do we have the scent of sulfur from the artesian well that supplies the water for the Rowley's house and pool. And they are faced with another maintenance problem—the build-up of algae that used to require emptying and scrubbing down the pool every two weeks. Maybe Dupont has since come up with an antialgae product. I must remember to ask Sam and Jane, though if I do they may think I am having a recurrent attack of smugness.

Other long-time friends of ours, Barbara and Clarke Wescoe, have a handsome free-form indoor pool in their house in Allentown, Pa. Glass walls separate it from the family room. In fact, the pool is so sparkly and the glass walls so clean that George walked right into the wall, raising both a welt on his forehead and his awareness that people in glass houses should post danger signs. But when we visited them one time we were surprised to see that the pool was empty. So were they. The water had leaked out and no one knew how or where. I never heard the solution to the mystery, but at that time the people in the house just below them were getting a bit apprehensive about

where all those thousands of gallons of water might turn up.

The pool trauma that was least bargained for and the least likely to happen again occurred at the Vaughan's pool in Cambridge, Vt. Their home is on a high plateau just under the brow of Mt. Mansfield. The view is magnificent and the pine trees crowd down to the edge of their fields and lawn. Along with the ubiquitous woodchucks, deer, skunks, raccoons, and rabbits that we all harbor, the Vaughans also have an occasional bear visiting them. They were aware of this when one raided their beehives and made off not only with the honey but the hives as well, ripping down the fence and sending the neighbor's cows high-tailing it in all directions.

One spring when the Vaughans were away and their son David was house- and dog-sitting for them, he heard the dog barking with unwonted fervor and was surprised to see a very large moose sauntering up the driveway. The moose was equally surprised and didn't share the Vaughans' enthusiasm for dogs. Their pool was still under its winter cover which looked solid enough to a scared moose but was not made to support 1,400 pounds. He crashed through the cover, his long legs reaching bottom over most of the area. His sharp cloven hooves not only touched bottom, they gouged the plastic liner thoroughly before he made his escape out of the deep end and took to the woods. I doubt if the average insurance policy has a clause for moose damage. He may be one of God's creatures, but you can hardly claim that his presence was an act of God.

A moose couldn't hurt our pool. We'd be delighted to see one down there. I'd prefer a moose to our woodchucks and raccoons any old day or night. It would restore a touch of wildness to a region that is becoming too domesticated. We have No Trespassing signs at the pool, but they are intended for two-legged creatures who often are illiterate. I wish the moose and deer could read. I'd add, "Anyone with paws or cloven hooves is welcome to drink, swim, or browse by permission of the owners."

Mr. Blandings, You Had It Easy!

When I was young and foolish I thought that the cautiousness of my parents (or anyone over forty) was based on lack of courage. Now that I can't even see forty over my shoulder, I realize that the young are not necessarily brave, they just don't know what they are getting into when they undertake a project. And a good thing too because if they did know they'd never poke a questing toe out of their sleeping bags in the morning.

The longer you wait, the more of your bizarre dreams you jettison. The chances that George and I will ever skip stones into the Atlantic (or is it the Pacific, or a little of both?) at Tierra del Fuego or be among the honored guests at the Nobel laureates' dinner in Stockholm are remote. But somehow we didn't consider building a small house in the country quite that much of a mirage. We thought that the deterrent was cash rather than courage. Lots of people build houses and live to tell about it. That should have warned us. Have you ever known anyone who built a house who didn't tell about it, and tell about it, and tell about it?

From the time we bought the farm in Jericho Center in 1948, we thought about where we might eventually build a

90

new house on the land. "The building site" for many years was on top of the hill where we could look off west to the Adirondacks and east to the Green Mountains. Doesn't everyone yearn to place his dream house on a hilltop either to lift up his eyes unto the hills or look down on his neighbors? But the fact is that a house on a hilltop is exposed to the rigors of winter, which in Vermont are very rigorous, and it requires a long driveway, which not only has to be paid for initially but also plowed out and sanded all winter and dried out every mud season forever after. Even the long walk to the mailbox seems more of a chore than a challenge when sleet is stinging your face.

So twenty-three years later the building site slid downhill and came to rest on a rocky ledge within sight and sound of the brook and only ninety-two nearly level feet from the road.

We returned to Vermont to become year-round residents. With the architect's plans drawn up in detail, the site approved, and the snow melted, we took off for Europe to visit our daughter Patty in Finland, expecting that when we returned home the eleven bids would be in and we would pick the most attractive. Alas we returned to find that only two builders were interested enough to bid on the house and that one of those bids was fifty percent higher than our estimate and the other ninety-five percent higher. So we backed away from the drawing board, paid the architect for his time and effort to date, and then whirled around like dying flies trying to find a prefab that we liked and could afford. It also would have to be made habitable before cold weather forced us out of the porous little old house that, in addition to imminent collapse, never has had central heating or winterproof plumbing.

Everyone will tell you that you should drill your well before you build your house. George told it to himself and everyone within earshot. But no one tells you what to do if your driller gets delayed for several weeks because of other jobs that took longer than they estimated, a broken drill that had to be replaced, and faulty underpinning on the rig. So six weeks after we had originally hoped to start building, when the concrete mixer arrived with its round revolving stomach full of ready-mix the day before the well driller, we were squeezed into letting him go ahead and pour the slab. The next day when the enormous red rig of the well driller snorted in and reared up on its hind wheels, I wondered what the well drilling would do to the hardening concrete. Innocent that I was, I worried about a crack in a sand castle when a tidal wave was about to demolish the whole beach. The first day we found the drilling rather exciting, all the gleaming steel and whining engines and the red-haired young man who operated the mysterious levers wearing a helmet to protect his ears from the trauma of his trade.

We told ourselves that we couldn't expect water *that* day. After all, they only went about 150 feet the first day, and our nearest neighbors had struck water at 185 feet. We generously guessed that it might be 200 feet before he would come running down to the house with the joyful news. At the end of the second day we were getting a little tired of the noise. Not that it was so loud down at the old house. It was that the sound began to resemble the clatter of chips being raked in by a croupier. On the third day, every time I heard the drill stop I catapulted up from the garden sure that they had struck water. Each time the lovely silence lasted only long enough to put down another length of pipe. By the fourth afternoon I invented errands to take me away—anywhere. By the fifth night George and I were both lying awake doing mental arithmetic. On the eighth day, at 643 feet, the driller told us he thought he and we were wasting his time and our money—$4,450 worth of a dry hole in the ground as deep as the Washington Monument. A pebble dropped into the shaft took 30 seconds to *plink-plink* down, ricocheting off the sides until it went *ploink* in a tantalizing splash of shallow water at the bottom.

The drilling rig pulled up its pipes, settled back on its six big wheels, and lumbered away. Another driller said that if we wanted him to he'd try at another spot in about six weeks! We didn't want him to.

Even with a ten percent discount for no water, we had already paid $4,000 for a dry hole, $1,000 to the architect for plans we couldn't use, a driveway and slab already in, which probably meant we owed another $2,000 to the builder. The only touch of comic relief was that the phone company appeared and installed a phone, which sat in solitary splendor on the concrete slab. Friends and neighbors commiserated. Jack Cross presented us with a fresh salmon he had just caught in Canada, and Clara Manor sent over homemade doughnuts. Our nerves and finances were fringed to the point where we explored all other alternative water supplies. Mr. Lanou Hudson and Mr. Paul Lanou of the Lanou Plumbing Company came out and volunteered their experience in rural water problems. Bob Carlson, the world's most cheerful county agent, a geologist and two self-styled dowsers all came and scrambled over the land with forked sticks, slide rules, measuring tapes, and sympathy.

We had known for twenty-three years that the land just below our old dwindling spring was always wet. But it took near financial ruin to convince George, and the two dowsers to convince me, that there was any volume of water there. A backhoe crawled around the house and bit out a 10 foot hole, put in three 3-foot tiles, and overnight this reservoir filled with 700 gallons of water! Of course it had to be piped up over a ledge of rock and 200 feet to the new building site, but the sound of running water and costs in the hundred instead of the thousands fell mellifluously on our battered eardrums.

Carpenters arrived at 7:30. There was the sound of pounding and progress, and the skeleton of the house rapidly took shape. In no time the roof was on and all but two windows were in. Two months later the same two windows had not arrived, and snow and winter winds were straining the temporary plastic. The wallboard went up and the taper taped all the seams and corners. It looked very neat for fifteen minutes until the taper had an argument with the builder, stalked off the job vowing revenge, slipped back after the other workmen left, ripped off the tapes and gouged out the corners with his knife.

Each day was a unique blend of an uncertain amount of progress and a certain crisis. The engineer from the electric company announced that the electrician had put in one box instead of two and that two were required. The lumberyard hadn't the faintest idea what had become of the two missing windows. The kitchen appliances were slow in arriving, and it turned out that they hadn't been ordered after all. When the transparent stain was applied on the outside of the house each of the panels came out a different color although the wood was supposed to be the same. As I walked up the driveway one morning I thought the front door looked funny, just about as funny as if someone had spilled a pail of dark brown stain all over it. Someone had—one of the boys had slipped with a can of mahogany stain, and the pale clear ash solid front door looked like a Rorschach test. The foreman announced he was sick and went into the hospital for three days of tests.

94

Two days later he showed up raging and muttering that he wasn't *that* sick and "nobody's going to make a guinea pig out of *this* baby!" The new taper didn't show up for two weeks, and the electrician and plumber were all tied up in someone else's wires and pipes.

Our beautiful, mild Indian-summer weather was suddenly turned off and the temperature dropped to ten degrees. Meanwhile, back at the old house with exposed pipes from well to pump and through unheated rooms to the one section we could heat with our senile kerosene stove, we became not only nervous but numb. George wrapped the hose from well to pump in a hot wire, and we left the faucet running in the bathroom. I wore two pairs of wool socks stuffed into George's fleece-lined slippers and only took off the slippers at night. If I sat down long enough to read, it was also long enough for my fingertips to turn whatever color precedes rigor mortis. Never underestimate dishpan hands. The only time my hands felt as though they were on the same arterial circuit with the rest of me was when they were lolling in the luxury of hot dishwater.

The workmen at the new house had two heating dragons they called salamanders. They looked, sounded, and smelled more like jet engines. But they breathed out such fiery fumes that one salamander reduced the workmen to tee shirts. So the other heater was hauled down to the old house and set up in the bare, unheated living room where in spite of its sinister appearance its conscientious thermostat told it when to erupt in flaming fury. This periodically filled the house with a simulation of an express subway roaring through a local stop, the smell of the round black kerosene heaters of my childhood, and the color and heat of the fiery furnace that never quite immolated Shadrach, Meshach, and Abednego. The salamander never quite immolated us either, but it was not the cozy sort of hearth at which one warmed hands and heart.

I set up and canceled dates with the carpet man and the mover so many times that they finally said, "Don't call us. We'll call you." Our neighbor, Joan Cross, invited us for "a bath and dinner," knowing that the great treat would be the bath. The ultimate luxury is submerging in a tub of hot water after several weeks of dabbing here and there with a washcloth in a room where your breath steams and a hot wash cloth turns into an icepack in the time it takes to lift it to your face.

The space heater was also a watchdog, even though there was nothing much to watch in the old house. All our household goods except for the bare necessities for summer living were in storage. One morning the gas supplier came to refill our cooking gas tank. With his truck engine and the pump that fills the tank running, he apparently didn't hear our monster roaring until he opened the door to put the bill inside. I saw him on the doorstep and dashed for the door to warn him. Too late! He opened the door, stared into the flaming circle of the heater, gasped, "What's *that?*" and leaped back five feet. Too bad the space heater in repose up at the new house didn't have the same effect on a weekend prowler. Sometime between Saturday afternoon, when we saw it, and Sunday morning, when we didn't, the other heater had disappeared. Tools were untouched, but the heavy, four-foot-long salamander was gone. So every morning the one at the old house had to be dragged through the snow up to the new house and then brought back each afternoon to keep our pipes from freezing overnight.

Deer-hunting season opened, and there were several days when there was no activity at the new house but the chickadees darting in and out of the pines. The foreman protested that nothing further could be done until the electric company put in the new pole. Each day the foreman, the builder, and I phoned the electric company and each day we were reassured that it would be done as soon as possible. Inasmuch as we had first contracted their engineer four months earlier, their speed was somewhat less than breathtaking. I finally described conditions at our old house, sparing them no details about my three pair of socks, the plastic taped over the windows, the newspapers tacked over the cracks, the congealing pipes. Whether this moving picture or the hope of respite from our barrage of phone calls finally turned the slow wheels of progress, a promise of a specific date for the installation of the electric pole finally came through. There was dancing in the driveway that night. There were lots of other things in the driveway too, scraps of plasterboard and lumber, milk cartons, coca cola cans and other lunch debris that the workmen tossed about casually, nails sprouting up like dandelions, and sheets of plastic blowing about like tumbleweed. The builder had warned me that a building site looked like a pigpen while the building was in progress. Our pigs would have been insulted— it looked like Coney Island on Monday morning.

Three days later the electric company arrived with two trucks and a beautiful new pole. When they assured me that my services were not required, I drove off to Burlington. When I returned at three o'clock I heard the ominous sound of a heavy motor racing and the whine of spinning tires. The big truck had driven around behind the barn to lift one of the men up to the old pole and was now stuck in the loose soil that had been recently dug up when the septic tank and pipes from the well were laid. It wasn't stuck in just any old loose soil. It was right over the new water line and was grinding down deeper and deeper squashing our brand new water pipes.

The tub was in place, but someone had forgotten to put in plumbing for the shower. The vanity arrived but when the basin was being installed it broke and a new one had to be ordered.

The kitchen sink, dishwasher, and stove were all lined up on the screened porch ready to be installed as soon as the kitchen cabinets were done. The foreman was supposedly building our kitchen cabinets at home. At least that was the activity the builder was paying him two weeks' salary for, but when at the end of three weeks neither cabinets or foreman materialized it became quite clear that unless I wanted to cook on the porch, wash the dishes in the bathtub, and stack them on the floor, we would have to buy readymade cabinets at once and the readier the better. With unaccustomed good luck in finding what we wanted in stock and the subtle pressure of wailing like a banshee, all the cabinets were delivered the next day. The builder and the electrician were merrily installing them the next day when they asked me what I had done with the sink. Now, if it had been installed and hooked up to the water supply I might conceivably have drowned myself in it but although I was lugging books, knickknacks, and clothes all over the place, I hadn't touched the sink. In fact, now that they mentioned it, none of us had seen it for several days. The package with the faucets was there, but the sink had either taken to the woods or become the victim of finger blight. Why anyone would steal just a sink has been added to our collection of unsolved mysteries.

Having reached the stage where I only believed what I could touch with my own two hands, I took off for Burlington again and lugged home another sink, telling myself all the way home that nothing else could go wrong that day because there wasn't much left of the day by the time I got back.

The next morning the carpet men were to come early, and

98

I had my nose flattened against the window pane watching for them. By ten thirty the appearance of both my nose and the window were suffering so I phoned to the carpet company.

"Oh, they left hours ago," the man cheerfully assured me, so back to my post at the window where I was rewarded by seeing the carpet salesman drive up, not in a truck stuffed with fat rolls of gold and crimson carpet and eager workmen, but just by himself stopping by to see how they were getting along. All morning I had been imagining what might have happened to them—lost, car trouble, delayed by another job. But even my frantic and fertile imagination could not have dreamed up what the salesman learned when he phoned the company. They had started out more or less on time, but the driver, who was also the one who knew how to install the kitchen carpet, was a Vietnam veteran who had had a traumatic experience overseas. When he was driving an army truck along a jungle road, the truck in front of him carrying his buddies, was blown up, killing all the men in it. Since that time if he drives a truck more than ten or fifteen miles away from home plate through wooded or lonely areas, he is overcome with anxiety, sweating, and nausea. His work is mostly in town and the boy with him, who knew the way didn't know about his problem until he became so ill that they had to take him back and spend the rest of the morning trying to find someone to take his place. Serious for the chap with the neurosis but, accustomed as we had become to a daily crisis, this one only had the distinction of being the least likely to be anticipated. The carpet men crawled around our floors until ten that night, and the kitchen carpet had to be laid another day by someone whose neuroses didn't show.

The missing two windows miraculously appeared a week before Christmas. There was a bad moment when the builder

99

thought one was too small, but it slipped into place with the aid of prayer and positive thinking, and I got up off the floor and dried my eyes.

It wasn't easy to convince the movers that the final moving day was at hand. They had grown quite attached, not only to our lares and penates but also the monthly check for storage.

The walls weren't painted. We were to do that ourselves at some later date, much later. The bookshelves weren't built for the same reason, but we turned off the kerosene stove in the old house and drained the pipes. Not a moment too soon. The very last night in the old house, the pipes froze, but luckily only the hose to the well, so that George was able to drain the inside pipes and shut off the electricity, feeling a bit guilty that we were abandoning a house that had sheltered us in the summer for twenty-three years. It would have been hard to leave in the summer but the thought of a hot bath, a washing machine, dryer, and dishwasher, luxuries that we had not enjoyed in months, sent us stumbling over the unpainted threshold, laden to the eyebrows, filthy, frostbitten but miraculously aware that this collage of timber and pipes and wires that had all the frustrations of a nightmare for the last three months seemed suddenly to have turned into a dream house after all.

September

The first few days of September are apt to be warm, and we are lulled by the illusion that summer is not over. I am not fall-conscious until the sound of the big yellow school buses lumbering up our back road startles me out of my summer reverie. All along the roads clusters of children, self-conscious in their new school clothes, giggle and jostle each other while waiting for the bus, and when it finally rumbles off with its noisy cargo the family dog at each stop looks wistfully after the departing leviathan, all too aware that his life has changed.

There are other unmistakable signs of fall—a flock of birds wheeling above the meadow and sweeping in a dark cloud over my head so suddenly that I can't tell what they are, starlings probably, the first splashes of scarlet light up the swamp maples, and a few yellow elm leaves float on the pool. This year there are no closed gentians at the edge of the brook. Did they get mowed down by mistake? I miss their lovely deep blue color, though I really think they should open up and be real flowers. They look unfinished, frozen into buds.

We dig the late potatoes in early September and cut open an apple to see if the seeds are brown. I love the spurt of tart juice when you bite into a not-quite-ripe MacIntosh. The Kennebec potatoes are unusually scabby this year. Maybe we'd better stick to Katahdin and the early Red Norlands. At this time of year we begin to worry about the first frost. There was just a touch of light frost on the 18th, which curled a few Zucchini leaves but didn't touch the fruit. But on the 28th we had a black frost. The temperature dropped to 24°. Thick white frost crunched under my boots when I rushed down to the garden to splash water on the lettuce, which I hadn't covered, before the sun should strike the garden. The eggplants were covered with grocery bags, but that wasn't protection enough. The first hard frost is so sad, always followed by warm days and wistful thoughts of "if only . . . ."

Our pumpkins are ripening late this year, hardly any color until the middle of the month. The Kentucky wonder beans were still producing by mid-September. They are so tall that I had to use a pair of long wooden tongs to nip down the last top ones. They are our favorite beans, so tender at any size, and if we plant them two or three weeks after we plant the bush beans we can enjoy beans for a full two months. When I try succession crops of the bush beans they sometimes all mature at the same time.

Goldenrod is beginning to tarnish, and the sensitive fern is chestnut brown. But the meadow is filled with pale lavender asters, and the deep purple ones are in clumps along the roadsides.

Last night a snowshoe hare got in the Hav-a-Hart trap. He was a young one, soft brown at this time of year, with big ears and large hind feet that didn't look especially like his winter snowshoes. He must have been more curious than hungry because the bait was cat food, calculated to lure a raccoon. Rabbits are supposed to be herbiverous, the dumb bunny! We took him way up the road into the wild woods of the Notch. The minute the trap was open he leaped to freedom and made off in great bounds, zigzagging first left and then right, instinctively trying to confuse his pursuers. Only we didn't pursue. We just stood and watched and admired and felt that awe which I always feel when I watch a wildling in the woods—the doe that stands still for a moment in the road before she bounds away, the shoe-button eyes of a raccoon, sizing you up and then waddling off into the underbrush. In that instant there is contact between the two living creatures, each wondering what the next move may be.

P-cat, our peach-colored kitten that the Manors gave to the grandchildren this summer, wants so much to be a house cat. We want her to be a barn cat, but she prefers people to the two pigs and seventeen laying hens in the barn. I don't blame her for avoiding the geese in the meadow. The few times she has slipped through the fence into their domain they have rushed at her with outspread wings and lowered heads, hissing ominously. When we are in the house she jumps on the window bird feeder and taps the window with one pink-mink paw. She is the only near-soundless cat we've ever had. Her mouth forms a "miaow," but it is inaudible. I know she has vocal cords because I tripped over her one day and the outraged squawk was loud and clear. Why *do* cats walk between your feet and weave back and forth in front of you indoors or out? And why don't we hear more about broken legs, hips, and wrists caused by cat-tripping? It's been a long time since we've had a cat, and we are wondering if she'll be a deterrent to our birds. We feed the birds all winter, more for our entertainment than for their nurture, and it wouldn't seem quite fair to lure them within P-cat's hunting territory.

This is the gossamer season. Milkweed seeds hover almost

motionless in the air, supported by their tiny shimmering parachutes. Cobwebs are traced in silver by dewdrops or frost. The mists that are tucked down over the river like a soft blanket in the early morning are brushed aside softly by the warm sun before noon. There is a portent of winter in the first frosts, but it is not to be taken seriously. There will be warm days ahead and wild colors, and tomorrow will take care of itself.

Out of the Mouths of Babes

If you want an opinion that is more candid than candied, spend some time in fourth- through seventh-grade classrooms. Somehow my name was included on a list of available—that is, free—speakers for a school "enrichment" program.

In the case of fourth- and fifth-grade classes a mother, pressed into service above and beyond the call of duty, would call to ask me, or a teacher might write me a note. The seventh graders picked a classmate who was proficient in both spelling and penmanship and gave her the duty. These notes were always on personal notepaper that had puppies on the front and faint pencil lines inside to keep the writing on neat rows. They were most formal. "Dear Mrs. Wolf, I have a request to make of you. We would like to have you come to our school and talk to us about your job as an author, about some of the problems you face and about the things that cheer you on. Please consider the matter." Well, these notes are some of the things that cheer me on, and so do the letters that children were required to write after my visit. I am gratful to their teacher for leaving the spelling and punctuation untouched and hope the printer will too.

"I really enjoyed your talk. It was more fun than other school. I have read your books and some were better than others. I read the one about the letters in the atic and the one about where the vetarian did something to the little boy pigs so they wouldn't get the little girl pigs preganet."

One little girl wrote wistfully, "I thought you have an interesting life. I wish I had an exciting life but I didn't and I suppose I never will." I wanted to assure her that there is life after twelve and that it would be more interesting to her than mine because she would be in the middle of it.

James wrote, "I think you had the moast exiting life of any Body I ever seen. I almoast die laughing at the goat with the raisins. Well, I better go. P.S. I think your a nice lady."

And from Judy, "Thank you for showing the seventh grade what you have found in your addick. It is fasanating. I like the one when your husband put the new tolet in and it brock and when your little girl said mommy the sheeps make raisins in the car I could have died."

Susan said, "Thank you for coming and talking to us about yourself. I like your books. They are sort of funny and sort of not."

And Dana's realistic approach, "I liked what you take about. I sore you could of take for an hour longer but we had to do some work and you probule had something beter to do." Not really, Dana.

But the most original creation was written by Deborah from Richmond. The date at the top of her sheet of lined paper was Dec. 12, 1402, followed by this poem.

> Roses are red
> Violets are blue
> Chickens are funny
> The letters were too!

106

Sugar is sweet
lemons are sour
you stayed for 45 minutes
Why not an hour?

Crackers are crumbly
the lightbulb was an invention
I wrote the phoney date
Just for your attention.

The most well-organized interview I have ever had was con-
ducted by fourth- and fifth-grade students in Burlington at
the opening of the Fletcher Free Library's new wing. It was
explained to me in advance by four small persons. They had
mimeographed sheets with a list of twenty questions they
had thought up, such as, "How do you spend your day from
when you get up?" They each asked a question in turn, and I
was instructed to "please answer them without saying a lot
because we gotta finish in twenty minutes." It was taped by a
fifth student, and the class photographer was also on hand.

But their sophistication broke down after my talk and they
gathered around to look at the old letters I had brought. One
little boy picked up my first book, written fifteen years ago,
turned it over, and studied the photograph on the dust jacket.
He looked at the picture and then came closer and stared at
me for several seconds. Finally he pulled on my sleeve and
asked, "Is this picture supposed to be you?"

"Yes, it is," I said, admiring the efforts of Bachrach on my
behalf.

"Well," he sighed, "you must have been a lot prettier in
the olden days."

The Empty Nest
Has a Silver Lining

It's hard for me to believe that I am the only parent who is finding happiness in the empty nest. Most of the literature implies that Mom hovers on the brink of depression when the last child packs up records and running shoes and heads for college or separate-but-unequal living quarters. I resent the assumption that I don't love my children if we don't live under the same roof. Nonsense! Frankly, I think the writers of these articles are either lying or trying to extend the image of the self-sacrificing mother beyond its natural life-span.

The truth is that most mothers are not born selfless—it is thrust upon them. Remember the cartoon in "Family Circus" where one toddler, whose ice-cream cone has fallen upside down in the sand, is comforted by his sister, who says, "Never mind, Jeffy, Mommy will give you hers?" Now that's what you do for about twenty years in the pursuit of your children's happiness. I did it too, and I honestly enjoyed those years not only because life was smoother that way but because I clung to the hope that if I was considerate and sensitive to the kids' needs, they might grow out of the "Me first!" (last and always) phase and turn out to be civilized adults. And they have more than justified my faith, but judging by the regressive behavior of our so-called civilization, maybe that's not an adjective to aspire to anymore.

We have two bright and beautiful daughters, two absolutely great sons-in-law, and three talented grandchildren. I love them all dearly, but I rejoice that our house is not their house. Just think, I can now finish my own ice cream cone! I can open my own birthday presents and answer the phone first. I know exactly where the car is, in the garage awaiting the pleasure of my company. Before our children were old enough to have licenses, my car was an unmetered taxi. In feeble defense let me say that we lived in the country too far out for them to walk or ride their bikes on their appointed rounds. Even though gas was only thirty-five cents a gallon, it wasn't that much fun to shuttle between scouts, music lessons, dentist appointments, and friends, both coming and going.

I can now shop for such "yukky" foods as shad roe, endive, "stinky" cheese, and chicken livers without hearing them compared unfavorably to hamburger, noodle soup, hot dogs, and bizarre flavors of ice cream. We can enjoy leisurely drinks before dinner without hearing "Aren't we ever going to eat?" and our mealtimes are dictated by our pleasure rather than the demands of cheerleading practice or lacrosse games.

Laundry needs to be done only twice a week, and it no longer contains unmatching socks, bleeding Madras, and overripe gym clothes. Years ago we had a neighbor who tried to phone his wife unsuccessfully for over an hour. Their home line was chronically busy. He finally sent a telegram. His teenage daughter had to hang up the phone to answer the door when the Western Union boy arrived. The message read, "Get off the phone! Love, Dad." We tried tirades and timers, but hanging up the phone is equivalent to cutting off life-support systems to a teenager. They can eat, drink, do their homework, and brush their teeth with the phone cradled between shoulder and ear. We had a thirty-foot phone cord. Debbie used to take it upstairs into her room at night, bury it under her pillow to muffle the ring and wait for a call from her ninth-grade boyfriend long after his parents and hers were asleep. Maybe that's why he became a lawyer and state senator. Debbie still makes lengthy phone calls, but when she began paying her own phone bills the phone came out of the closet.

The greatest myth is that the childless nest is empty. The two-parent home, while perhaps an endangered species, is once again the chummy nest those two people chose to build together in the first place. The chance to resume a closer and less fragmented life with your husband is the unheralded bonus. The sound of the Rolling Stones is no longer heard in our land. The gravel in the driveway is not constantly crunching with the comings and goings of cars both foreign and domestic. We watch our choice of TV programs, dance to the Big Band songs, and can kiss or even yell at each other without embarassing the children or convincing them that Reno is the next stop.

Who needs the so-called empty nest? I do and I'll bet you do too. Is it so weird to love your children and your husband enough to value their independence as well as protecting your own?

October

October should be called Calliope in honor of the chief of the Muses, for what is more evocative of their creative arts than a blue and gold October day? The air is as tangy crisp as the apples that are weighing down the branches with their ripe burden. And the call of October is as strident and loud as a circus calliope, a clarion call that evokes in us some atavistic response as stimulating as adrenalin.

Every day we look into a kaleidoscope of tumbled and mixed colors that form changing patterns. Some sugar maples turn many colors on the same tree, one side still green, a patch of golden edged with scarlet, another peach colored, and another flame red. The ashes also have green mixed with purple. The blueberries and euonymus are vibrant with rose, crimson, and vermillion. The saffron and lemon and apricot arches of tree tunnels or sugar maples actually seem to give off light. But the "popples" are clear, one-colored primrose yellow in sharp contrast on the hillsides to the dark green pines, "navy green" Debbie used to call it, a perfect foil for the bright yellow and reminiscent of the aspens and pines in the mountains of Colorado.

Driving through New Hampshire on our way to Boston, we marveled at the garnet oaks, deep wine colors of burgundy and claret. It is almost impossible for a Vermonter to concede that New Hampshire might excel in anything, but I have never seen such wine-dark oaks in Vermont. Our oak saplings have that color, but the mature trees seem to turn brown rather than ripe red.

October smells of ripe apples, the inside of a pumpkin with the seeds, and pulp slipping between your fingers. Is there anything in the world harder to grasp than that stringy membrane? Everywhere there is the smell of wet leaves, that scent half-ripe and half-decaying, somewhere between sweet and musty, and the occasional spicy scent of chrysanthemums.

October tastes good, too, because it is the peak time for all the fruity flavors of Concord grapes, apples, pears, plums, and fresh cider. It is the season for rich pumpkin soup, fragrant with onions, celery, and thyme; hearty beef stews, laced with red wine and a wonderful meal-in-a-bowl mixture we like made with sauerkraut, kielbasa, pork, onions, white wine, potatoes, carrots, and a bit of gin or juniper berries; all those stick-to-your-ribs stews and chowders that fill the house with mouth watering scents. The last batch of piccalilli gets put together at the end of October, using up the last green tomatoes and peppers.

In spite of a reputation for October's bright blue weather, the month is full of contrasts. The morning mists that are tucked protectively over the valleys soften the bright foliage colors to opaline tints, and the warmth of noon on an early October day is drowsy. Flies buzz and whirl on the window sills in their frantic dance of death. Wasps hum, a chain saw whines far up in the woods, and the birdsong is muted. It is Keats's "Season of mists and mellow fruitfulness."

Just as suddenly, toward the end of the month, a storm rips through, tearing the bright leaves off the trees, pelting the roof with rain or even hail, swirling the falling leaves in mini-cyclones. The wind shrieks and rages. Dead branches fly through the air. The highways are as slippery with wet leaves as they will be later with ice. But it is a mock tantrum, and the next day may dawn clear and still, with the sky a blue more intense than at any other season, with all the colors that sang and shouted from the treetops now spread beneath the bare branches, glistening wet and glowing like the rich colors of an oriental rug.

What Do You Mean, "Silly Goose"?

We fully intended to serve one of our first geese for Christmas dinner, but we found one excuse after another until we finally admitted that we were chicken when it came to geese. Why? Well, they have a certain dignity and presence. With a few exceptions a chicken is just a chicken but a goose is an individual. He looks you right in the eye with his own dark brown ones, and that is the undoing of the executioner. Why do you suppose they blindfold prisoners who are sentenced to death? Not for the prisoner's sake I am sure.

Even though we are relatively new at geese tending, we are already chauvinistic about them. We have four African geese, and that hardly qualifies as a basis for scientific observation and definitive conclusions, but in comparison with other creatures we have known for thirty years, geese aren't nearly as silly as our chickens or our sheep. And for sheer silliness to the point of imbecility, our turkeys win wings down. An overenthusiastic dog or a low-flying helicopter will spook a turkey flock. They may pile up in a corner trampling each other to death in the same way that humans have been known to behave while trying to escape from a burning night club or circus tent.

A chicken is also a bird of little brain. They will resist being caught and put in a crate, but when you open the crate they will refuse to come out and have to be pried out flapping and shouting in fowl language about police brutality.

But back to the geese. I've consulted with other geese people about the attributes and shortcomings of their geese, and not one has called them silly. The adjectives they use range from "clever," "curious," "courageous," "smart," to an occasional "aggressive." None of the geese people I have questioned has wanted to kill and eat their geese. Anita Haviland admitted that the first year they killed one. Never again, and they now have one that's been with them for fifteen years.

We got our first two geese from Thelma Wheeler when they were a month old before they had developed the distinctive chocolate brown stripe down the back of their necks. They were very shy with us but immediately attached themselves to our two sheep, and the four of them moved around their pasture as though controlled by radar. They ate each other's food and slept together, two wooly lumps and two apparently headless mounds of feathers. The Feitelbergs' goose carries togetherness farther than that. She sleeps on the ewe's back!

Two geese did not a gaggle make, so we didn't see the flock behavior that Thelma Wheeler describes. When the ice breaks up in the Wheeler pond, all the geese follow the leader into the water. When the snow was high enough near the fence they followed him over the fence into the road where the salt had melted the snow into a few inviting puddles. When she went to the door and clapped her hands they all waddled back over the fence like guilty children caught in the neighbor's cherry tree. The males argue over who will be the leader, but when one is chosen, they all follow him without further dissent. One seasonal source of argument among the Wheeler's geese is the crop of small misshapen apples from an old apple tree. The limbs hang low to the ground, and in the fall the geese practically climb the tree to pick the apples and to fight over them. As soon as one has an apple in his beak, the others try to get it away from him. We weren't aware of the affinity of geese for apples until we threw some drops into the feeding pan for the sheep. The geese rushed over, wings outspread and necks stretched forward "squonking" their delight, and snatched the apples out from under the sheep's muzzles. When Gail Feitelberg wants to lure her peripatetic goose back into the pasture she uses an apple as the most effective lure.

Anita Haviland, who is a goose person of long experience, chats with her geese and they have provided a good many Mother Goose and Gander tales. One day when she was painting her bathroom she set the mirror outdoors propped up against a ladder. One of her ganders came up to pass the time of day and began to talk to the goose he found in the mirror. He would try to touch the reflection, then back up and try again, apparently enamored enough to try to woo it with his mating dance. Finally in frustration he went behind the mirror to find where the goose really was and when he found nothing but the ladder, uttered a mournful cry of unrequited love and flew back to the flock.

The Haviland geese and their bantam hens use a hay-filled packing case for a nest. The Havilands collected the banty hens but left the goose eggs hoping they would be hatched. It was the banty hens however, rather than the mama geese, who proceeded to brood the goose eggs. Each banty hen could cover only two goose eggs, and the sight of ten little bantam hens all over each other trying to cover twenty goose eggs looked like a miniature pile-up on a football field. The geese

116

apparently appreciated the baby-sitting services of the surrogate mothers and preened the banty hens during their confinement. When the eggs began to hatch the geese came honking, their maternal instincts activated by the whistling of the goslings, claimed their babies, and took them away. One gosling who seemed to be having difficulty breaking into the world was taken into the house where he was kept for five days as a pet. Two that were day-olds were kept indoors over night. When the parent geese outdoors heard the goslings whistling they came right over to demand the release of their children. When the babies were brought out the geese rushed to them bowing and goose-talking. The day-olds went right to the old geese, but the five-day-old didn't acknowledge his gooseness and fled back to the protection of the humans. Finally, Anita bowled him gently into the middle of the gaggle. The gosling panicked in terror, but the geese formed a circle around him and deprogrammed him until he was convinced that he was a goose after all.

Gail has goose tales also. They have a pet ewe and a pet goose who is the ewe's best friend. When a neighbor brought over his gander hoping to mate it with Gail's goose, the gander went through all the courting maneuvers, dancing, and bowing, but the goose was unimpressed. When he made amorous advances the goose ran under the ewe for protection and the ewe butted the gander away, making it quite clear that she was feminist enough to insist on the right of choice for her friend.

No such crisis has arisen in our meadow. Our first two geese were content to graze with the sheep. They recognized our truck and announced our return running to meet us with wings outstretched, squawking hoarsely in greeting.

The Wheeler's African geese take snow baths when their pond is frozen over. Ours don't have access to a pond, but they love to squat in their water pan, which is just wide enough to hold a goose. In the winter this waterer has an immersion heater to keep the water from freezing. On a cold morning passing motorists do a double take when they see a goose sitting in a large flat pan with wreaths of steam coming up around her. No, we are not cooking our goose.

On the last day of the Winter Olympics the Feitelbergs and their son settled down to watch the deciding hockey game. Gail fed the animals much earlier than usual, but when their accustomed feeding time came the goose flew out of the pasture for the first time ever, came up to the house, and knocked on the door. When she was ignored she came to the back window where she could look in and see them and knocked and squawked, making it very clear that they were derelict in their animal husbandry. Since that day she flies out of her pasture at exactly her feeding time, goes to the garage where the feed is kept, and hammers away at the container, not just any container, the goose grain container!

When the time came for their goose's ewe-friend to drop her lamb, the goose got very upset and became such an over enthusiastic midwife that they had to be separated. The result was that the goose felt the lamb was a rival for the ewe's affection, and they had to keep them apart for the lamb's safety. This year Gail is considering allowing the goose to be with the ewe during her confinement in the same encouraging role that fathers now play in the new birthing suites in the hospital.

When our ewe went into labor our geese paid no attention, but after the lamb was born the geese appointed themselves guardians for the lamb with all the officiousness of English nannies. For the first time they became aggressive, hissing and pecking at me when I tried to make friends with the lamb.

Our two geese began laying in the first week of April. George had provided an open shed for them but also filled an old tire with straw and placed it under a wild grape vine. They ignored the shed but loved the tire nest. We have kept laying hens for years but found it unnerving to discover a huge white goose egg weighing more than six ounces tucked under the straw in the tire. It was better than an Easter egg hunt. After two weeks of laying our geese became broody even though we had taken away the eggs each day. You couldn't lure them off the nest with their favorite grain. Even though we provided them with a second straw-filled tire, they both crowded together overflowing the original nest. When we moved the sheep, geese, their feeders, and nests to a fresh pasture the two geese squeezed themselves back through the fence and squatted on the bare spot where their nest had been. Finally George had to string chicken wire along the strip of fence between the two pastures, and after a day of poking their heads through the chicken wire and flapping their wings wildly they gave up and accepted their new pasture. But they never accepted the new location of the nest.

They stopped laying when they became broody, but when we added a gander his introductory macho behavior, strutting, spreading his wings, honking loudly, and bossing the girls around, must have activated their hormones because they started laying again. With the hope that those eggs might be fertile, we left them undisturbed, and the two geese embarked on their long incubation period of thirty-one days. Fortunately, once he had established his dominance the gander apparently no longer felt the need to strut and attack the other geese. He still attacked the sheep if they approached the grain feeder. Their wool was thick, but they skittered away from his fierce beak. I shared their reluctance to argue with him on any subject.

The geese rarely left their nests to feed or take a drink of water. On one of those few occasions we saw that there were two eggs in one nest and three in the other. A week later we got another peek. One nest was empty and the other had only one egg. There were only one or two small scraps of shell. Would a raccoon eat shells and all? We never found out but our hopes for a gosling clung precariously to one possibly fertile egg.

A month and a few days after the gander's arrival date the lone egg still was motionless. Nothing happened the next day or the next, and I began to believe our goose egg was really a zero. But the following morning I passed them on my way to the garden, and there was a ball of yellow fluff waddling along on outsized orange feet, flanked on either side by his proud mama and aunt. All three adult geese hovered around him constantly. No human was allowed to approach him, but in their enthusiastic guardianship they often stepped on him eliciting a tiny outraged squawk. He ate the adult geese's grain and drank water the first day and swam happily in their flat waterer with no instruction from his relatives. In two months he was full grown, his baby yellow down replaced by the faun-colored feathers and chocolate brown stripe of African geese.

The next year we took five eggs to Thelma and Jack Wheeler's incubator. Because we are not sure that our gander is purebred African (he has a yellow bill and yellow eye rings), I marked our eggs "Half-breed, Wolf-Goose," anatomically impossible, but it did distinguish them from the Wheeler's pure-bred eggs. Of the five only two hatched, and the Wheelers kindly kept them in their brooder and gosling yard for several weeks. When we brought them home both George and I had misgivings about their safety if we put them in with our two geese and our fierce-eyed gander. We kept them in an enclo-

sure in the garage for a week in the feeble hope that a little more growth would make them more able to fend for themselves, we faced up to the fact that sooner or later we would have to try them out with the adult geese. We carried them down to the pasture and I held them while George went inside the pasture armed with a broom in case the geese attacked the goslings. At the sight and sound of the goslings the geese rushed over and I gingerly set down one gosling at a time near them. With beak open and tongue vibrating in a hiss the gander stretched out his neck and charged, not at the goslings but at George! He continued his dire threats until George retreated a few steps. Meanwhile the two geese were bowing and greeting and talking softly to the babies. This was an instant family, and they cruised off together, the gander in the lead and the goslings, flanked protectively by the two geese, waddling along behind.

If I had consulted Katrina Stokes before this happened, I might have known there would be instant bonding. Katrina's gander takes his parenting very seriously. When the goose lays an egg he does everything short of handing out cigars. He squawks and screams and announces to the world that his very remarkable wife, with his able assistance, has laid a platinum egg. When she sits on the nest he settles down nearby and softly sings a little lullaby. He does not seem to feel that his macho image is threatened by an occasional turn on the nest and can tuck an egg under his goose-down vest protectively with the best of geese.

John Vivian, who has written extensively about geese, says that a goose is the only animal he has seen kill a skunk and I know that our cat never ventures into their pasture. Is it true that geese will rid a barnyard of snakes? We only know that we see far fewer snakes than we did before we became goose-herds. That may be a myth, but geese were considered sacred in Egypt 4,000 years ago. When the Gauls attacked Rome in 390 B. C., a detachment climbed up the Palatine Hill so silently that the first man was unchallenged, but on climbing over the rampart he disturbed the sacred geese, who awoke the garrison. Marcus Manlius rushed to the wall and hurled the unfortunate fellow over the precipice. To commemorate this the Romans carried a golden goose in the procession to the Capitol every year. Chauvinistic as we may be about the attributes of our local geese, I've yet to see a golden image in Jericho Center. But with the growing coterie of geese people in our area it wouldn't surprise me to see a Jericho-Underhill delegation goose-stepping along Route 15 in the next Memorial Day parade.

November

Like the rear end of a cow ambling down the road ahead of you, legs, udder, and tail all swinging arythmically, November has very little to recommend it visually.

Grays, browns, and the winter green of conifers are relieved only by the white trunks of the birches or the tamaracks' golden spires. After the conflagration of color in October, November seems too hushed, too monochromatic under too consistently leaden skies. It is always just above or below freezing, which, until the snow blankets the landscape, feels much colder. November is dull days to be tolerated rather than celebrated, days to be gratefully pushed behind you.

Now if I found excitement in football or deer hunting or election day I might look forward to the hysteria of those late-fall activities, but I think all three of them are boring too. When we lived in Kansas I was supposed to be thrilled that we were entitled to seats on the fifty-yard line for all the K.U. football games. Everyone else seemed to enjoy shivering and shrieking and sitting in the car for two hours while 40,000 people in 10,000 cars inched their way out of the parking lots. But we endeared ourselves permanently to a few friends by giving them our tickets and our grateful (but unspoken) blessing. My attitude in Kansas toward football was as heretical as my attitude toward deer hunting in Vermont. I guess I just don't like to be that cold or stiff or confused.

Like childbirth, the best thing about November is that it feels so good when it is over. But the fact is that if you like a four-season (five in Vermont) climate as I do, the contrast is essential to set off the special pleasures of each season.

No Floridian could get as excited as I do over the first snowdrop. The scent of lilacs and apple blossoms might go unnoticed in the tropics. And if our maple trees were aflame all year long, we might long for the soft beige browns of the desert or the lush green canopy of a rain forest. My Aunt Edith, who was transplanted from South Dakota to California, used to yearn for a cool gray day with the rain drumming on the roof.

November is a vestibule with the doors closed both behind it on the warmth and color of October and still shut off from the white mantle of December. The Canada geese, the hounds of heaven, are arrowing south, the essence of wildness in their calls. The beaver is shoring and storing his lodge and food supply for the winter. The trees have shed their leaves to reduce the loss of moisture through respiration, and the cows and horses still in the fields are shaggy in their winter coats. A cat on a porch railing condenses into a ball to conserve heat, and we in Vermont bank sawdust or hemlock boughs or tar paper around the bases of our houses, put up the storm windows, and move the pumpkins indoors.

We start to feed the birds again, and the chickadees and woodpeckers and bluejays, our fair-weather friends, swarm back and stuff themselves on suet and sunflower seeds. And speaking of stuffing, Thanksgiving adds some welcome warmth to November. We no longer raise turkeys, but we do try to

get a fresh Vermont one. It seems a time to get back to funda-
mentals, so we make our own cranberry sauce and mincemeat
and pie crust; the potatoes, onions, and squash are all from
our garden.

Perhaps that is what November is about—getting back to
the essential shape of things. We see the trees as they really
are, a neighbor's house that was hidden by summer foliage,
the church spire that is only visible in winter. It is a time to
look at the structure of things, the rugged shape of an oak
tree, the symmetry of a woodpile, and the cinnabar of dried
weeds. A warm house becomes a home in November, a warm
haven from the cold and rain.

Let's Talk Turkey

With Thanksgiving looming ahead of us and the elections mercifully behind us, it is time to talk about that celebrated bird. In the first place, a turkey is really a pheasant, and he never had anything to do with the middle eastern country of the same name. He is a native American, which would entitle him to run for president on the unlikely chance that he could live to the required age. I seem to recall that a presidential candidate or two has been called a turkey, by the opposition, of course.

Our Thanksgiving bird, who would also have been our national bird instead of the bald eagle if Ben Franklin had had his druthers, got his name through mistaken identity. Christopher Columbus was so gung ho for India that he not only named our native American Indians, but he named the unfamiliar wild fowl he found "Tuka," which is what peacocks were called in India. A turkey's size and gait are similar to those of a peacock even though the male plumage is less spectacular. Maybe he thought he was only seeing the female of the species. My acquaintance with peacocks is limited to those in the zoo or a few presiding over the lawns at Warwick castle, so I don't know if peacocks are equally stupid. I do know from personal experience that a turkey is a bird of little brain, who has to be taught to eat and then can't be taught much else. We raised turkeys for a few years until we decided that the only thing dumber than turkeys are the people who think it would be fun to raise them.

They do look nice, not en masse, but a few strutting around the barnyard looking down their beaks at lesser creatures lend a bucolic ambiance. And of course they taste great, but so does swordfish and I'm not planning to raise them.

It wasn't long before New Englanders had hunted the wild turkey into local extinction. In fact, as late as 1950 it was reported that the wild turkey no longer existed in Canada and the northeastern United States. But wild turkeys are tough, in the regenerative rather than the culinary sense, and now they have staged a comeback and are plentiful enough so that we have a wild-turkey hunting season. I've never seen one in his natural habitat, but then I've never seen a bear in these hills either though we have neighbors who unwillingly supply bears with both honey and an occasional lamb.

Our native turkey looks more or less the same as it did to Columbus 500 years ago or when it was introduced to the Pilgrims at that first three-day spectacular in 1621. Audubon wrote that in the early 1800s an unplucked turkey weighing ten to twelve pounds might sell for three cents, and a twenty-five-to-thirty-pound bird brought a quarter of a dollar. That would now buy a third of a pound of dressed turkey, but of course the new broadbreasted turkeys have more meat and less plumage. In 1973 there was a seventy-five-pound turkey reported in Utah, but it didn't say what became of him or who had an oven roomy enough to hold it. Let's see, a seventy-five-pound turkey would serve 125 people, and even though

128

I've grown accustomed to the gathering of clans at Thanksgiving, 125 souls and especially that number of bodies is carrying togetherness too far.

Oddly enough, the largest turkey farm is not in the United States but in England, where one turkey farm raised 5,400,000 birds. I can't picture 5,000,000 anything anymore than I can comprehend the millions of miles from here to Saturn and I'd rather not. The National Wild Turkey Federation, which is dedicated to the progress of reintroduction and management, now has a membership of 30,000. They don't say whether the membership is human or fowl. I prefer to think they mean human and while we're talking turkey, let's think in terms of just one human family and one unfrozen, succulent Vermont bird, a hen of about fourteen pounds, roasted to the color and sheen of a horse chestnut, redolent with sausage, celery, and onion stuffing, its fragrance perfuming the house on Thursday.

Now there is something to be thankful for! It could have been the other way around with the turkey's image imprinted on the quarter and guess what served up on the Thanksgiving table, the bald eagle.

And Then There Were None

We hold one bucolic truth to be self-evident. Turkeys are not bright. You would think that having learned this and given up on turkeys in 1961, the sound of the gobbler would no longer be heard in our land. That's what you'd think if you overestimated the intelligence of Wolfs. With that knack of allowing the disastrous experiences to sink back into the dim recesses of our subconscious, twenty years later, there we were, hurtling along in our pick-up truck with a box containing three loudly peeping poults anchored securely between my knees.

A turkey poult is not an object of beauty. It looks like a scrawny miniature vulture, and any size vulture is a minus ten. In fact, most new-hatched birds look as though they should have been incubated a little longer. They are all skin and stubble, with outsized feet and beaks. Of course, baby ducks are enchanting and so are chicks and goslings, but most wild birds are plain ugly at first and the turkey is not that far removed from the wild.

But our triumvirate was vocal and lively and they had learned to eat, which is a major achievement for a turkey poult. A human baby nurses instinctively and so do most mammals.

Chicks and ducklings will pick at everything and in the process sort out what is edible, but a turkey poult has to have his ugly little face shoved into his feed until he discovers that he likes what he sees. It is a wonder they survive in the wild, but I suppose they learn by imitating Mama who struts and pecks her way through the forest.

The four-week-old poults cost $3.75 each. The waterer and the feeder came to $5, and 25 pounds of feed was $3.75. Total initial investment equals $20. Add another 200 pounds of feed at the minimum, and the total cost would be $33. On the way home we surmised that each turkey would dress out at about 14 pounds so while 78¢ per pound is about the same as what they would cost at the supermarket in November, we convinced ourselves that the object was not economy but the superiority of the product. Besides, the fresh Vermont turkeys usually do cost quite a bit more than the frozen birds not locally grown. Statistics are always used to make whatever point you wish to promote, and financially sound husbandry in our case is often beside the point.

We housed them in a large wooden box with chicken wire over the top through which they could poke their silly heads and survey their environment. Their environment at first was the garage, partly for warmth and also because George had not quite finished their raised pen in the woodshed, with a wire mesh floor and chicken wire side. This allowed them to peer out myopically at the cars passing on the road, and it also allowed their droppings and the enormous quantity of feed they spilled to fall through onto the earth floor of the shed. We felt pretty smug about the whole thing. The turkeys seemed relaxed and happy and so were we. All went well for several days and nights. The turkeys whistled and we smacked our lips in anticipation of Thanksgiving three times next year.

131

Do you remember the rhyme "Ten little Indians, all in a line. One went away and then there were nine"? One morning instead of three little turkeys there were two. No sign of a battle, no commotion that we had heard, and only a few feathers under their raised coop as slim evidence of a kidnapping. Whatever had absconded with one of our turkeys had climbed up the frame of the coop then scaled four feet of chicken wire and dropped down into their coop. And to make off with the turkey he'd have to carry it in his mouth, retrace his perilous ascent of the undulating chicken wire wall, go down the other side, and shinny down the post to the floor. Is a fox that much of a climber? Our best local climbers are raccoons so we put the blame on the masked bandit.

Two nights later another little Indian bit the dust, and now there was one. Certainly we couldn't leave him there as exposed as a sitting turkey. So back he came to the wooden box in the garage. I don't recommend keeping any domestic fowl within olfactory range of the house. When we had kept turkeys in the past and housed the day-olds in the cellar for six weeks our whole house had a fowl odor. One lone bird seemed reasonably happy in his box. We changed the newspapers under him every two days and kept him well supplied with feed, grit, and water. He feathered out nicely, although his cramped quarters wore his tail feathers ragged. He spent most of the time with his head thrust up through the chicken wire supervising whatever was going on in or near the garage. He became agitated when the garage doors were opened or shut, but then so do I. They make a horrendous metallic racket. Each night the garage doors were closed and each morning, whether or not we were planning to use the car, the doors were opened to give him a wider horizon and to dilute the essence of turkey in the air. George lugged wire and lumber up from the barn and planned to construct him a completely enclosed pen the next day.

That night we forgot to shut the garage doors. In the morning the feed and water was spilled and the box was empty. Two small spots of blood and three feathers were in the driveway.

One little Indian standing all alone. He went away and then there was none. So there you have the brief tale of three turkeys. Don't bother to tell me that those thirty dollars would have bought two fresh, oven-ready Vermont turkeys next November. The way we feel about raising turkeys right now, the next dollar spent on turkeys will be right at the checkout counter at the supermarket.

December

Our five-year-old grandson, Patrick, who lives in Finland, could hardly wait for December last year because he wanted to open the little windows of his four advent calendars. Of course he had already opened every one of them several times, but not legally. On the first of December he could really open December 1 and leave it open. In Finland on December 6, their independence day, candles twinkle in every window. At that time of year the night is very long in Finland. It is dark by half past three in the afternoon, so children coming home from school in the dark and people returning home from work see the soft flickering streamers of candlelight shining on the snow and remember the quiet strength that has kept Finland free. At least, as Debbie used to say, December has something to look forward to.

December 1980 was the coldest I ever remember. Degree-day units soared and so did the heating bills. It was lucky that there was a lot of snow to insulate some of the pipes from the deepening frost levels. Many nights it was twenty below zero, and on Christmas night it sank to thirty-two below at our house. Cars wouldn't start and gas lines froze on the highways.

The snow squeaked underfoot, and there was frozen fog in the air, not snow but a mist of tiny crystals. Cold that intense is threatening. You know it is potentially lethal. You could quickly and easily freeze to death if not properly protected.

A whipped-cream blanket of steam hung over the lake and in spots where there was open water on the Winooski river, little columns of steam rose from the water that at thirty or forty degrees was fifty degrees warmer than the air. At night as the temperature sinks the roof makes sudden shotlike noises and the windows are so thick with frost patterns by morning that you can't see out to read the thermometer. Just as well. Besides there are natural thermometers that indicate the cold very clearly. The rhododendron leaves are curled and drooping to save transpiration and so are the pine needles. Any cat who is brave enough to be outdoors sits gathered into herself to preserve body heat.

There is something ominous about such intense cold. It reminds you that a human is a tender bit of protoplasm in a potentially hostile environment. But after the wet and gray of November, December can be beautiful, with smooth, untrampled expanses of snow sparkling in the sun under a bright blue sky. Snow clinging to the evergreens, a Christmas-card scene out of every window. The birds are fluffed up fat, and they look shaggy because the tiny muscles that produce our goose flesh have raised each of their feathers to trap the warm air near their bodies.

The birds at our feeders are a constant source of entertainment in December. Twelve to eighteen evening grosbeaks squabble and swoop, and two or three bluejays add to the colorful mobile. Chickadees dart and flutter in a continuous effort to maintain their accelerated metabolism. Even though our geese are naturally equipped in the best, and most expen-

135

sive, insulating material, goose down, it is incredible that they tolerate this cold outdoors. They stand on one flat orange foot with the other one tucked up in their feathers or they sit on both feet and tuck their heads under their wings. One very cold day we felt they really should be protected so we herded them, protesting, into a stall in the barn for the night. The next morning they rushed outdoors eagerly. P-cat, however, could not be persuaded to set a velvet paw over the doorsill even when lured by a full feeding dish. Of course, the food froze instantly so I had to bring it in anyway.

One night when George turned on the outside light, he motioned for me to come and see the tiniest deer mouse scurrying around on the snow under the bird feeder, gleaning the dropped sunflower seeds. Not more than an inch and a half long with a round humped little back, white underparts, bright eyes, and outsize ears, it caught sight of us and dove down one of the tunnels that the red squirrels make under the snow.

At the check-out counter of the supermarket, in the line at the post office, filling the tank at the gas station, the cold becomes the local common denominator.

"Twenty-eight below at my house."

"Our thermometer read thirty-four below at six o'clock."

"Man on the radio said it was thirty-eight at Newport."

It becomes competitive, a matter of pride in endurance. The Vermonter is just contrary enough to challenge the elements and exult in his ability to survive. Stamping into the gas station, ears ablaze and beard whitened with frost, a gnome of an old man quips, "Airy, ain't it!"

November is monochromatic, but December is full of color contrasts. There is an assortment of bright rubies, barberry, high-bush cranberry, and the wine-red cones of the sumacs. The green of the evergreens and the Venetian red of Vermont

136

barns are more intense against the snow, and the long blue and mauve shadows toward dusk contrast sharply with the golden light of the setting sun tinting the white farmhouses pale yellow.

Christmas in the country still has a Currier and Ives look. We cut our own tree in our woods, dig out the old ornaments remembering earlier Christmases. Shabby red stockings are still hung by the chimney with care if not with the same anticipation of childhood, and we eat our own goose and homemade plum pudding for Christmas dinner. And of course the brandy didn't flame properly as usual even though I did warm it first. But modern technology has some good points too. We were able to dial directly to Patty and Tage in about one minute. Across 6,000 miles and seven hours time difference, Peter's sleepy little three-year-old voice brought him right into my lap. Patrick was already asleep because, although it was 2:30 P.M. here, it was 9:30 P.M. there, and they had just returned from a long Christmas Eve celebration at Tage's parents' home.

Silent night, holy night, late evening in Kerava, Finland, lengthening shadows in Jericho, Vt. Sleep in heavenly peace, little grandsons everywhere, in Pakistan, Jerusalem, and Belfast. At least for tonight and with hope for the new year, Peace on Earth, Good will toward men!

CHRISTIAN HERALD ASSOCIATION AND ITS MINISTRIES

CHRISTIAN HERALD ASSOCIATION, founded in 1878, publishes The Christian Herald Magazine, one of the leading interdenominational religious monthlies in America. Through its wide circulation, it brings inspiring articles and the latest news of religious developments to many families. From the magazine's pages came the initiative for CHRISTIAN HERALD CHILDREN'S HOME and THE BOWERY MISSION, two individually supported not-for-profit corporations.

CHRISTIAN HERALD CHILDREN'S HOME, established in 1894, is the name for a unique and dynamic ministry to disadvantaged children, offering hope and opportunities which would not otherwise be available for reasons of poverty and neglect. The goal is to develop each child's potential and to demonstrate Christian compassion and understanding to children in need.

Mont Lawn is a permanent camp located in Bushkill, Pennsylvania. It is the focal point of a ministry which provides a healthful "vacation with a purpose" to children who without it would be confined to the streets of the city. Up to 1000 children between the ages of 7 and 11 come to Mont Lawn each year.

Christian Herald Children's Home maintains year-round contact with children by means of an *In-City Youth Ministry*. Central to its philosophy is the belief that only through sustained relationships and demonstrated concern can individual lives be truly enriched. Special emphasis is on individual guidance, spiritual and family counseling and tutoring. This follow-up ministry to inner-city children culminates for many in financial assistance toward higher education and career counseling.

THE BOWERY MISSION, located at 227 Bowery, New York City, has since 1879 been reaching out to the lost men on the Bowery, offering them what could be their last chance to rebuild their lives. Every man is fed, clothed and ministered to. Countless numbers have entered the 90-day residential rehabilitation program at the Bowery Mission. A concentrated ministry of counseling, medical care, nutrition therapy, Bible study and Gospel services awakens a man to spiritual renewal within himself.

These ministries are supported solely by the voluntary contributions of individuals and by legacies and bequests. Contributions are tax deductible. Checks should be made out either to CHRISTIAN HERALD CHILDREN'S HOME or to THE BOWERY MISSION.

Administrative Office: 40 Overlook Drive, Chappaqua, New York 10514
Telephone: (914) 769-9000